THE ESSENTIAL BUYER'S GUIDE

ROLLS-ROYCE/BENTLEY

SILVER SHADOW
T-SERIES

Including Corniche, Camargue, Silver Shadow II &

Bentley T2: 1965 to 1995

Your marque expert:
Malcolm Bobbitt

VELOCE PUBLISHING
THE PUBLISHER OF FINE AUTOMOTIVE BOOKS

www.veloce.co.uk

First published under ISBN 978-1-84584-146-1 in March 2008 by Veloce Publishing Limited, Veloce House, Parkway Farm Business Park, Middle Farm Way, Poundbury, Dorchester, Dorset, DT1 3AR, England. Reprinted January 2014 & April 2018.
Tel 01305 260068/Fax 01305 250479/e-mail info@veloce.co.uk/web www.veloce.co.uk or www.velocebooks.com.
ISBN: 978-1-787113-40-4 UPC: 6-36847-01340-0

Readers with ideas for automotive books, or books on other transport or related hobby subjects, are invited to write to the editorial director of Veloce Publishing at the above address.

British Library Cataloguing in Publication Data – A catalogue record for this book is available from the British Library.
Typesetting, design and page make-up all by Veloce Publishing Ltd on Apple Mac.
Printed and bound by CPI Group (UK) Ltd, Croydon, CR0 4YY.

Introduction & thanks
– the purpose of this book

The Silver Shadow and T caused a storm when they were introduced in the autumn of 1965, for they took the revered names of Rolls-Royce and Bentley into a new era. Bristling with technology, and designed in accordance with the most modern car-making methods, the Silver Shadow and Bentley T consigned traditional Rolls-Royce manufacturing practices to history. The stunningly modern and, arguably, less ostentatious Rolls-Royce appealed to a much wider, and noticeably younger, clientele than before.

With total production of the Silver Shadow exceeding 40,550 vehicles, a figure nearly twice that of the previous model built at Crewe, the new model secured Rolls-Royce's fortunes for the future.

Manufacturing methods might have changed with the Silver Shadow and Bentley T, but happily Rolls-Royce's legendary attention to detail did not. That the cars still appear fresh after more than forty years is a tribute to the efforts of Rolls-Royce Chief Stylist John Blatchley and his dedicated team. Because of its purity, styling changed little during the cars' fifteen-year production run, the essential format continuing to grace the Corniche until 1995.

Today, the Silver Shadow and Bentley T are sought-after classics which promise many years of driving pleasure. This is where this book comes into its own; for within the following pages there is everything you need will to know when contemplating a purchase. A vehicle's grand image might initially influence a decision to buy, but a

The imposing front profile of the Silver Shadow.

superficial check could easily miss problems, leading to disappointment and additional expense. Using this book when evauating a potential purchase will help you avoid such pitfalls.

Thanks

The author is grateful to Rob Jones, Benver Services (Crewe); Martin Bourne; Andrew Minney; John Bowling of Bowling Ryan; Michael Hibberd; the Rolls-Royce Enthusiasts' Club; Sir Henry Royce Memorial Foundation; Alex Wilson; Rodney Timson; Terrence Quinn; Bill Wolf; and the owners of Silver Shadows and Ts who allowed me to photograph their cars. All photographs are from the author's collection unless otherwise credited. Cover picture courtesy Klaus-Josef Rossfeldt.

The Bentley T shared the Silver Shadow's bodyshell, but portrayed a more sporting image. (Courtesy Rolls-Royce)

Essential Buyer's Guide™ currency

At the time of publication a BG unit of currency "●" equals approximately £1.00/ US$1.42/Euro 1.15. Please adjust to suit current exchange rates.

Contents

1 Is it the right car for you?
– marriage guidance

Tall and short drivers
Electrically-operated seats provide optimum adjustment.

Weight of controls
Steering is light, but on early models is noted for its vagueness. Smooth and powerful braking.

Will it fit in the garage?

Model	Length (max) dimensions	Width
Silver Shadow/T	16ft 11.5in (5170mm)	5ft 11in (1800mm)
Silver ShadowII/T2	17ft 0.5in (5194mm)	5ft 11.75in (1820mm)
Variations		
Long wheelbase saloons (Series I)	17ft 3.5in (5270mm)	5ft 11in (1800mm)
Long wheelbase saloons (Series II)	17ft 4.5in (5296mm)	5ft 11.75in (1820mm)
North American SSII	17ft 3.5in (5270mm)	5ft 11.75in (1820mm)
North American SWII	17ft 8.5in (5397.5mm)	5ft 11.75in (1820mm)
Corniche	17ft 3.5in (5270mm)	6.0ft (1830mm)
Camargue	16ft 11.5in (5170mm)	6ft 3.5in (1918mm)

Interior space
Ample!

Luggage capacity
The boot has 18.2cu/ft usable space.

Running costs
Servicing should be carried out at 6000 mile (9600km) intervals, though vehicles subjected to short runs should have engine oil changes at 3000 mile (4828km) intervals. Fuel consumption averages between 11 and 15mpg (25.7 and 18.8lt/100km).

Driving a Rolls-Royce is immensely satisfying. (Courtesy Rolls-Royce)

Usability
Wonderful in town, on motorways, and the grand tour.

Parts availability
Bentley Motors, through its 'Crewe' parts scheme, offers an excellent service, as do the enthusiasts' clubs and marque specialists.

Parts cost
Tyres, exhaust systems, bumpers, engines, transmissions, air-conditioning and hydraulic components are horribly expensive to repair or replace.

Insurance
The enthusiasts' clubs offer special insurance terms arranged through leading brokers. Insurers catering for owners of classic cars may offer agreed value terms.

Investment potential
Cars in pristine condition, especially Bentleys and coachbuilt variants, command high values.

Foibles
Vagueness of steering on early models.

Plus points
Sumptuous luxury.

Minus points
Running costs can be enormous.

Alternatives
Mercedes-Benz 450SEL 6.9 litre; Daimler 5.3 litre Vanden Plas; BMW 733i; Aston Martin Vantage, Volante; Lagonda; Cadillac Seville; Bristol 411, 412, 603; Jaguar XJ12.

Feeling comfortable with one's Bentley is important! (Courtesy R-REC/ SHRMF)

2 Cost considerations
– affordable, or a money pit?

The best policy is to pay as much as you can afford to acquire the finest car possible.

Service schedules
Bentley dealership main service (30k miles) ●x2000; independent specialist (24k miles) ●x500-900; 48k mile service ●x2000

Mechanical parts
Clutch (fitted) c●x900
Torque converter ●x400-600
Rebuilt engine c●x7000-7500
Piston ring set c●x400
Rebuilt gearbox c●x1200
New gearbox ●x3250-3500
Tyres (ea) (Avon/Michelin) ●x400
Hubcaps (ea) non-vented ●x100, vented ●x170
Brake discs (pair) ●x400-550
Brake pads (pair) ●x100-200
Handbrake pads (set) ●x55-60
Brake master cylinder ●x150
Brake callipers (ea), front ●x120, rear ●x350
Exhaust system (mild steel) ●x800; stainless steel ●x1100
Radiator ●x400
Alternator ●x250-500 (conversion ●x850)
Air-con unit (compressor) c●x650, blower motor c●x350, servo ●x500, actuator motor for heater flap ●x100-150
Water pump ●x250
Door window electric motor ●x550 complete with accessories
Head gaskets (pair) ●x80
Steering box, LHD ●x670; RHD ●x650
Steering pump ●x400
Steering rack, LHD ●x600; RHD ●x500
Starter motor Lucas ●x280; Nippon Denso c●x450
Fuel pump ●x400-500
Self-levelling accumulator spheres ●x250
Height control valve ●x300
Height control valve shaft ●x150
Height control ram ●x300
Height control solenoid ●x150
Shock absorber, front ●x380-550
Shock absorber, rear ●x300-650
Front spring ●x200
Rear spring ●x200
Trailing arm kit (pair) ●x350-1000 according to type
Fuel tank ●x500

Body parts

Headlamp (ea), inner/outer sealed beam ●x30; inner/outer halogen ●x60
Front wing, flared/non-flared ●x1100 according to model
Rear wing ●x350
Chrome body mouldings (wings, door and bonnet) c●x150 (average price)
Sill ●x75-100
Door (used) c●x350, but allow for reconditioning
Door mirror SS1/T1 ●x190; SSII/T2 ●x550
Windscreen ●x450 (1000 for Corniche)
Rear screen ●x1500 (900 for small screen, LWB model)
Radiator shell (new) c●x1000 (●x4000 complete)
Bumper, front, SSI/T c●x1250; rear ●x1150; SSII/T2, front c●x1900, rear
c●x2050
Front panel (valence) ●x400
Rear panel ●x300
Floorpans, front ●x400; rear ●x600
Boot lid c●x400 (1000 MPW)
Full respray c●x7000-10,000
Full pro restoration c●x50,000-75,000
Interior re-trim c●x9000-11,000
Body shell ●x7500-9000

Used parts

A number of specialists provide used parts either reconditioned or recycled. Always check that the supplier offers a warranty.

Publicity photograph depicting the Silver Shadow on introduction in1965. (Courtesy Rolls-Royce)

The Bentley T2 is a rarity compared to the Silver Shadow II. (Courtesy Andrew Morris)

3 Living with a Silver Shadow/T
– will you get along together?

Because of their imposing presence, Rolls-Royce Silver Shadows and Bentley Ts command attention and evoke a sense of respect. These vehicles, whilst exuding luxury and refinement, are meant to be driven, and, as such, are drivers' cars. Whilst some owners derive satisfaction from simply having one of these cars in the garage, fulfilment comes with keeping it in regular use. It will, even from a fuel consumption point of view, be an expensive car to run, but could prove all the more costly if used only very occasionally, with the result that components fail due to lack of use.

Chassis numbers
A chassis number is the key to a car's positive identity, particularly as there's a propensity for owners to have personalised registrations, thus it's not unusual for a car's registration number to change at various intervals throughout its life. A typical Silver Shadow or Bentley T chassis number may appear as:

```
      S   R   H   1   2   3   4   5
or    L   B   X   2   3   4   5   6
Key:  a   b   c   d   d   d   d   d
```

Key to identification
a: body type. S = Standard Saloon; L = Long Wheelbase Saloon; C = Two-Door Saloon (and Convertible up to chassis 6632); D = Convertible from chassis 6646; J = Camargue.
b: marque. R = Rolls-Royce; B = Bentley.
c: steering position. H = RHD; X = LHD. (From 1972, North American cars were given a special numbering system, X being replaced by a letter: A, 1972; B, 1973; C, 1974; D, 1975; E, 1976; F, 1977; G, 1978; J, 1979; K, 1980; L, 1981. From 1980, cars with fuel injection destined for California were given a 'C' suffix).
d: chassis serial numbers of four or five digits (in batches). Series 1: 1001-4548; 5001-5603; 6001-8861; 9001-26708; 30001-41648. **Series II:** 50001-50776 (Corniche and Camargue with mineral oil hydraulics).

Good points
Getting behind the wheel is a rewarding experience, and one can only savour the craftsmanship that went into building these cars. Driving the car is totally satisfying, with an abundance of V8 power and delightfully light, yet responsive, controls. Imperceptible gear changing and soft suspension, aided by hydraulic self-levelling, affords an exquisite ride under all conditions. Acceleration and braking is smooth without being in the least discordant, a quality made possible only by constant evaluation and improvement during the vehicle's development.

There's ample space for four adult passengers and their luggage. Air-conditioning is so sophisticated on later models that it can be controlled to give different temperatures at feet and face level. The build quality is such that cars are highly durable, and the finish of the paintwork when leaving the factory means that most vehicles will have maintained their prestige appearance for much longer than some other high quality cars.

There is excellent parts availability, and many Bentley dealers as well as autonomous marque experts provide a first-rate service by way of servicing and restoration. Moreover, the Rolls-Royce Enthusiasts' Club maintains records of all Crewe-built cars. Such was Rolls-Royce's commitment to perfection that the factory kept details of each car's interior specification so that the hide, veneers, and soft fabrics could be matched if required.

Bad points

These are big cars and care needs to be taken when negotiating narrow and twisting lanes. Likewise, parking can be problematic. Sadly, cars such as these can attract malicious attention when parked in the open.

Cars, particularly Silver Shadows, are often purchased purely for the status the name and R-R monogram affords. These cars may not always be treated to proper servicing schedules and will be discarded once the novelty of ownership has worn off. This tendency is less common now that the cars have reached classic distinction, though a vehicle with a long list of owners in succession might be one to regard with suspicion.

Open the bonnet and you'll find an engine compartment filled to capacity and bristling with technology, a sight bound to discourage the DIY mechanic. Component access can be difficult, and replacement parts are often expensive, as is routine servicing that, more often than not, requires specialist attention.

General view of the Silver Shadow.

Lush interior of a late model Corniche drophead coupé.

11

4 Relative values
– which model for you?

All Silver Shadow and Bentley T four-door saloons enjoy a uniform character and will at first glance appear similar. Variations, such as long wheelbase and coachbuilt models, will affect values.

  All values given are in relation to the models shown with 100% value.

Silver Shadow I, 1965-1970, 6.25-litre   50%
Silver Shadow I, 1970-1977, 6.75-litre   60%

'Compliant' suspension and radial-ply tyres introduced from 1972, wheelarches flared from 1974, and electronic ignition from 1975.

Silver Shadow Long Wheelbase (LWB)   50%
Silver Shadow II, 1977-1980, 6.75 litre   75%

Automatic air-conditioning specified.

Silver Wraith II (Long Wheelbase)   70%
Bentley T 1965-1970, 6.25 litre   70%
Bentley T LWB   70%
Bentley T, 1970-1977, 6.75 litre   70%
Bentley T2, 6.75 litre   80%
Bentley T LWB   80%
Corniche, 1971-1976   80%
Corniche, 1977-1980   85%

Bosch fuel injection introduced in 1980 for coachbuilt cars, except in California.

Corniche Convertible, 1971-1988   85%

Fuel injection for all markets.

Corniche II, 1986-1989   85%
Corniche III, 1990-1991   90%
Corniche IV1992-1995   95%
Corniche S, 1995   100%
Bentley Corniche, 1971-1976   90%
Bentley Corniche, 1977-1985   95%
Bentley Continental, 1985-1995   97%
Bentley Continental Turbo, 1992-1995   100%
Camargue   85%

The Pininfarina Camargue was designed around the Silver Shadow platform and running gear.

Camargue interior is different to that of the Silver Shadow.

Rolls-Royce Silver Shadow II with Bentley T2.

The Corniche has different rear styling to that of the standard saloon.

Preparing a Silver Shadow II for sale at the Beaulieu Autojumble.

Bentley T2 frontal styling. Silver Shadow and T bonnets are not interchangeable.

The Silver Wraith II is the long wheelbase variant of the Silver Shadow, thus affording rear seat passengers more space.

5 Before you view
– be well informed

When contemplating the purchase of a Silver Shadow or T-series car, there are many facets of a car's history to consider. To avoid a wasted journey, and the disappointment of finding that the car doesn't match your expectations, it will help if you're very clear about the questions you want to ask before you pick up the telephone. Some of these points might appear basic, but when you're excited about the prospect of buying your dream classic, it's amazing how some of the most obvious things can slip the mind. Also, check the current values of the model in which you're interested in the classic car magazines (these often give both price guides and auction results).

Where is the car?
Is it going to be worth travelling to the next county/state, or even across a border? A locally-advertised car, although it may not sound very interesting, can add to your knowledge for very little effort, so make a visit – it might even be in better condition than you expect.

Dealer or private sale
Establish early on if the car is being sold by its owner or by a trader. A private owner should have all the history, so don't be afraid to ask detailed questions. A dealer or marque specialist may have more limited knowledge of a car's history, but should have some documentation. You may be offered a warranty/guarantee and finance, but you must explore the limitations before committing to a deal.

Cost of collection and delivery
A dealer may well be used to quoting for delivery by car transporter. A private owner may agree to meet you halfway, but you should only agree to this after you've seen the car at the vendor's address to validate the documents. Conversely, you could meet halfway and agree the sale, but insist on meeting at the vendor's address for the hand over.

Viewing
It's always preferable to view at the vendor's home or business premises. In the case of a private sale, the car's documentation should tally with the seller's name and address. Arrange to view only in daylight, and avoid a wet day. Most cars look better in poor light or when wet.

Reason for sale
Do make this one of the first questions. Why is the car being sold? How long has it been with the current owner? How many previous owners?

Left-hand drive to right-hand drive/specials and convertibles
The vehicle chassis number will indicate whether the car was built with left- or right-hand drive, also whether saloon, coupé or convertible. If there is evidence of any conversion work it can only reduce the value. Treat the vehicle with suspicion

and ask to see documentation substantiating the modification. If there is no documentation, and the vendor is unable to supply information, it's best to walk away from the deal, unless this is the car you specifically want.

Condition (body/chassis/interior/mechanicals)
Ask for an honest appraisal of the car's condition. Ask specifically about some of the items described in Chapter 7. A car in a dilapidated state, or one having evidence of accident damage, is unlikely to be a profitable venture as remedial work could be extremely expensive.

All original specification
An original equipment car is invariably of higher value than a customised version.

Matching numbers/data/legal ownership
There's only one way to positively identify a Rolls-Royce or Bentley, and that is by the chassis number. The owner's handbook shows chassis, engine and body number, paint code and upholstery colour. Do VIN/chassis, engine numbers and license plate match the official registration document? Is the owner's name and address recorded in the official registration documents? For those countries that require an annual test of roadworthiness, does the car have a document showing that it complies? (An MoT certificate in the UK can be verified on 0845 600 5977.) In the UK, should the vehicle be the subject of a Statuary Off-Road Notice (SORN), the vendor should make this clear at the beginning of discussions and, if necessary, have the vehicle recommissioned. If a smog/emissions certificate is mandatory, does the car have one? If required, does the car carry a current road fund licence/license plate tag?

It's not uncommon for Silver Shadows and Ts to wear personalised or customised plates; ask whether the plate is included with the sale because, if not, arrangements will have to be made to have the vehicle re-registered with an age-related index number.

Does the vendor own the car outright? Money might be owed to a finance company or bank – the car could even be stolen. Several organisations will supply the data on ownership, based on the car's license plate number, for a fee. Such companies can often tell you whether the car has been 'written off' by an insurance company. In the UK the following organisations can supply vehicle data:

HPI – 01722 422 422
AA – 0870 600 0836
DVLA – 0870 240 0010
RAC – 0870 533 3660
ABS – 0800 358 5855

Other countries will have similar arrangements. The appropriate enthusiasts' club may well be able to assist.

Should you consider the car to be stolen you should report it to the authorities. The AA, RAC and ABS can also help, see telephone numbers above. Your local Trading Standards Office can also be of assistance, and the telephone number will be listed in your telephone directory.

Unleaded fuel
On all models use one of the recommended additives.

Insurance
Check with your insurance broker for details of cover before setting out, your current policy might not cover you to drive the car if you do purchase it.

How you can pay
A cheque/check will take several days to clear and the seller may prefer cash. However, a banker's draft (a cheque issued by a bank) is as good as cash, but safer, so contact your own bank and become familiar with the formalities that are necessary to obtain one.

Buying at auction?
See chapter 10 for further information.

Professional vehicle check
A number of organisations will undertake a professional examination of a vehicle and, if required, produce a written report. Contact a marque specialist who will confirm whether they provide this service. Marque enthusiasts' clubs may well be able to provide this undertaking, as will the AA, RAC or ABS. Before committing to such an arrangement ensure that you have precise details of the service, and the fee charged.

Before viewing, establish the vehicle's provenance. A car built to a particular specification will have the appropriate documentation; ensure that a customised example has been properly constructed. (Courtesy Bill Wolf)

6 Inspection equipment
– these items will really help

This book
Reading glasses (if you need them for close work)
Magnet (not powerful, a fridge magnet is ideal)
Torch
Probe (a small screwdriver works very well)
Overalls
Mirror on a stick/rod
Digital camera
Notebook or recording device
A friend, preferably a knowledgeable enthusiast

Before you rush out of the door, gather together a few items that will help you work your way around the car. This book is designed to be your guide at every step, so take it along and use the check boxes in chapter nine to help you assess each area of the car. Don't be afraid to let the seller see you using it.

Take your reading glasses if you need them to read documents and make close inspections. A magnet will help you check if the car has any filler, though will be of no use when checking the boot lid, doors and bonnet top which are formed from aluminium alloy. Be careful not to damage any paintwork.

A torch with fresh batteries will be useful for peering into the wheelarches and under the car. Fixing a mirror at an angle on the end of a stick/rod may seem odd, but you'll probably need it to check the condition of the car's underside. Take a digital camera so that later you can study some of the areas of the car more closely; take pictures of any part of the car that causes you concern. Ideally, make notes in a notebook, or use a recording device, and should you have a friend who is knowledgeable about these cars, or cars in general, let them accompany you – a second opinion is always valuable.

Vehicles that have been restored will require careful inspection. On this Series I Silver Shadow the mouldings along the sills are missing.

Before arranging to view a potential purchase, you should have ascertained whether the vehicle will fit your budget, have a shrewd idea of the car's condition, and know the exact model.

An early Silver Shadow, photographed for publicity purposes. (Courtesy Rolls-Royce)

In respect of your budget, it has to be remembered that the youngest saloon you are going to view will be approaching thirty years of age, and, unless the vehicle has been subject to recent restoration, there is every likelihood that some money will have to be spent on the car in the foreseeable future. As a general guide, therefore, take the asking price and deduct £2000 as a means of arriving at a negotiable figure.

Exterior

Your first impressions of the car being viewed are most important as they could largely influence the outcome of the purchase. The vehicle should be standing level with the ground, and to gauge this correctly look at the chrome sill moulding. If the car has an apparent droop to the rear, suspect tired suspension – the hydraulic self-levelling should adjust to weight differences within the car, i.e. the addition of passengers or filling the petrol tank. The hydraulic system should be depressurised, the engine having been at rest for some time and, therefore, cold.

Walk around the car and note whether the doors fit correctly. They should appear to fit flush with the coachwork, and any gaps or distortion should be noted. Check that the doors hang properly and that the lower edges are level. The doors should open and close without difficulty. With the doors in the open position, take a moment to inspect the condition of the door rubbers. Any splits in the rubber seals, especially those attached to the rear

A late Bentley T2 in concours condition. Series II vehicles have 'safety' bumpers.

edge of the front doors, can make opening and closing difficult, and rectification will prove an expensive operation. Take a note, too, of any corrosion in the vicinity of the chrome mouldings, especially where the fastening clips attach to the bodywork.

Silver Shadows and Bentley Ts are vulnerable to decay around the wheelarches and along the bottom edges of the front and rear wings. Don't be surprised to see evidence of repair work here, but do look for work that has not been competently undertaken. Repairs to the wing bottoms and wheelarches, if properly executed, should not reveal signs of paintwork having been rubbed down.

Now it's time to examine the boot. Be suspicious of a musty smell coming from the luggage compartment, and, with the lid in the open position, take a look at the seal, which should be in place and in good condition. A tell-tale sign that the battery has at some time leaked acid, or the area surrounding the battery box has been subjected to acid fumes, is the surrounding carpet showing signs of rot. The carpet which covers and surrounds the battery box should not be damaged or split. Check the condition of the battery, and beware of any signs of acid contamination or electrolyte leakage. Also, check that the box containing the car's hand tools is in place, and that all the tools are there and in good condition.

A car should stand level with the ground, shut lines should be even, and doors should have no evidence of deformation.

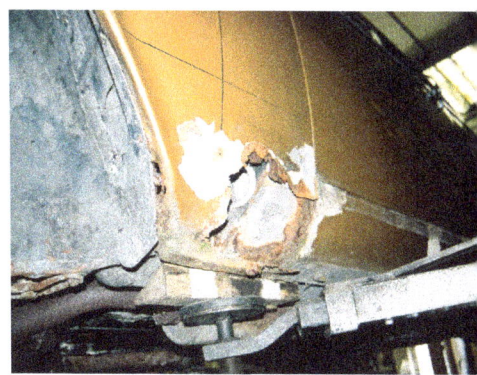

Front wheelarch and sill corrosion to this extent would deter most people from buying this car. Repairs are possible, but at huge expense!

When examining the tyres, look further than merely checking the depth of tread. With cars built before 1972, there is a tendency for tyres to wear on the inside edge. Tyre wear on cars with compliant suspension, i.e. built after 1972, is often most noticeable on the outer edge. Evidence of the former is quite usual and there should be no concerns about undue problems with the suspension system. What should be a matter of concern is feathering of the tyres, which could indicate that attention to the car's suspension is needed. Naturally, none of this information is relevant if the tyres are brand new, but this should prompt you to ask why the tyres were replaced, and how many miles they had covered.

Replacing a windscreen can be a costly exercise, and, therefore, it's wise to check for any cracks or stone chip damage to the glass. Evidence, too, of a diffused or opaque edging to the glass should be treated with suspicion, and could indicate problems leading to renewal of the screen.

The bumpers will also require investigation. Series I models have chrome bumpers with overriders, and damage is expensive to repair. In particular, look at the

The battery is located in the boot, and would normally have a protective cover.

Beware badly fitting or damaged bumpers; they're horribly expensive to repair and replace.

chrome quarter-sections and ensure there is no evidence of rust. Series II cars have bumpers with a moulded polyurethane insert; again, damage will be expensive to correct.

Under the bonnet

First impressions are very important. Although the engine bay of a Silver Shadow or T appears somewhat intimidating, there are clues which give an indication as to the car's condition. The flexible trunking should be free from splits or damage, and, while this might not pose a major problem, it is, nevertheless, costly to replace. Make sure that there are no signs of water leakage from the radiator or header tank, the tell-tale sign being the remnants of anti-freeze, particularly around the round cover on the top of the header tank. There is little more to do at this stage other than to check the condition of the engine oil by inspecting the dip-stick,

Under-bonnet trunking should not be split or damaged.

and to generally appraise the cleanliness or otherwise of the engine compartment.

Interior

Now it's time to take a look at the interior of the car. Yet again first impressions count, but it's important to look beyond the lush carpeting and leather seating. The carpets should be your first area of inspection. Water leaks from the windscreen are common and should not present a problem as long as they have been addressed in good time. Water leakage that has not been remedied will result in the front carpets rotting at the edges. The carpeting has a thick foam underlay which will absorb moisture, and there is also a waterproof membrane which will prevent the dampness rising to the surface of the material. In the event of a water leakage not being addressed, there is a danger that the moisture-laden underlay will cause the floorpan to rot. A vehicle showing signs of decay in this area should be treated with caution, the repair being very costly.

When inspecting the seating don't be put off by normal wear marks in the hide.

Some owners tend to give their cars regular treatment of 'hide food', which, when overdone, can result in the material taking on a hard, plastic feel. Check the condition of the driver's seat; it should be comfortable and supportive.

There is an air of opulence about even a well worn car, but be careful to take a critical look at the facia and door cappings to see whether the lacquer covering the veneer is in good condition. Any lifting of the lacquer, or indication it has turned a pale opaque colour, indicates that remedial (and expensive) work is necessary. Is the general state of the interior acceptable? Is it clean and cared for, even though having a natural patina, and is the cabin headlining clean and stain free?

Mechanicals and test drive

By this stage you should know whether the vehicle warrants further examination. Starting the engine from cold will reveal any inappropriate sounds coming from it. Don't be concerned about initial tappet noise, this should go away once the engine is warm. Look beneath the car for evidence of serious oil leakage.

With the engine running make sure the window lifts on all doors operate properly. The dials and gauges should also be operational, though on older cars there is a need on occasion to gently tap the instrument. The electric seat adjustment is usually quite reliable, even on older vehicles, but it's worth checking that everything works. Operate the headlights, sidelamps and rear lighting, the direction indicators, and, with the vendor or some other person at the wheel operating the controls, check that the brake and reversing lights illuminate. Having familiarised oneself with the controls and adjusted the driving position, it's time to take the car for a test drive.

Unless you're accustomed to a Silver Shadow or Bentley T, it's probably best to let the vendor conduct the initial driving. Listen carefully for any undue noises from the engine or drivetrain, and watch for any apparent difficulties in getting the car underway. Gear changes should be smooth, and there should be no evidence of knocking or rattles from the suspension. Excessive axle whine would be cause for concern, but don't worry about a gentle axle sound under 30mph. Let the driver take the car up to 60mph, all the while observing any inappropriate sounds or sensations from the vehicle.

When you're happy to take the wheel, put the car into 'drive' and gently build up speed until top gear is selected. The three-speed gearbox should be very smooth, but if the car is an early model with the four-speed automatic box, accept that gear changes will be perceptible.

Decrease speed to around 25mph. There should be negligible vibration or wobble through the steering wheel, but if there is, you should check two areas: firstly, the tyres for uneven wear; and secondly, the brakes. Vibration through the brake pedal could indicate a problem with the rear braking system. Increase speed to around 60mph and apply the brakes as if having to pull up sharply, but not an emergency stop. Any juddering from the car will indicate a potential problem with the front brakes.

To check the condition of the rear suspension on 'compliant' cars, it's useful to release the throttle when travelling at around 30mph and then to re-apply the accelerator. Do this several times and treat with suspicion any knocking of the rear subframe against the body of the car. If this is apparent there will also be a clunking sensation, indicating the compliant mounting units are worn.

Finally, on this brief test drive it's important to check that all the instruments and controls operate efficiently. Does the parking brake hold the car sufficiently? When travelling above 30mph engage cruise control, if fitted – applying the brake pedal should disengage the speed control automatically, and it should re-engage on applying the resume button. Does the air-conditioning work? Do the ventilation apertures operate? Operate the windscreen washers and two-speed wipers. Don't forget to try out the audio system; does the loudspeaker balance work? Now it's time to look at the armrests fitted to the front doors, they are adjustable for height as well as fore and aft movement. Check that the cigar lighters operate, that all interior lighting illuminates, and that the door handles and catches are in working order. Some of the latter items might seem academic on a car that is nearly 30 years old or more, but it does help to give an overall assessment of the vehicle.

Having concluded the test drive it's time to take another look under the bonnet. With the engine warm, ensure there are no signs of oil or water leaks, nor evidence of burning oil.

Paperwork/ownership/legality

At this stage of negotiations you should have established that the vehicle is everything it is claimed to be. You will have seen the registration documents and have examined the roadworthiness/MoT certificates, the latter confirming the mileage as indicated on the odometer. Beware that some owners take shortcuts over servicing, believing that a vehicle of such quality does not require as much attention as some other cars. Nothing could be further from the truth! Examine the service handbook to establish that correct service schedules have been maintained at the required intervals, and that the record is complete with dates and work carried out. Ask to see documentation for repairs; a vendor with a genuine car to sell should have every detail available.

8 Key points

– where to look for problems

When buying a Silver Shadow or Bentley T there are six major points to consider:

Exterior coachwork condition
Interior condition
Service history and documentation
Under-bonnet condition
Under-body condition
Roadtest

A brief survey of the coachwork will reveal any serious faults, such as corrosion around the wheelarches, along the sills, and in the vicinity of the trim mouldings. Check the carpeting for water absorbed in the underlay.

To examine the car's underside properly it will be necessary to have the vehicle raised on a ramp. Decay around the wheelarches and along the sills will be all the more apparent, and it's essential to check the floorpan for evidence of repairs, re-plating, etc. Check the front footwells for signs of rust coming from inside the car.

Test driving the car should reveal no major problems. Buying a vehicle that requires serious attention is bound to disappoint, it will be difficult to sell on, and expensive to repair. Don't let the vendor talk you into believing any problem is inconsequential, and don't allow the badging or the status of the marque to sway you. Don't let your heart rule your head!

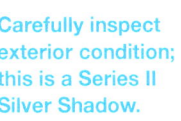

Interior furnishings should be in good condition and veneers should show no sign of damage or an opaque effect. (Courtesy Rolls-Royce)

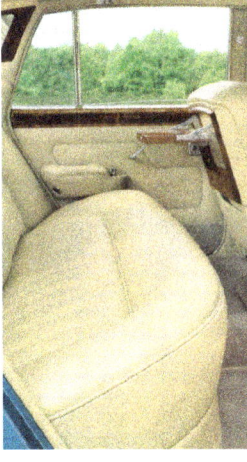

Carefully inspect exterior condition; this is a Series II Silver Shadow.

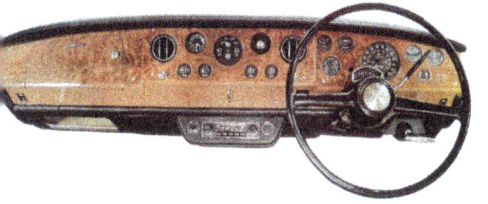

The interior condition of a car says much about previous ownership. The facia of an early vehicle before introduction of the 'safety' dash in 1969. (Courtesy Rolls-Royce)

Check external trim as well as the condition of the boot.

Look for evidence of even minor corrosion which, left unchecked, can become serious.

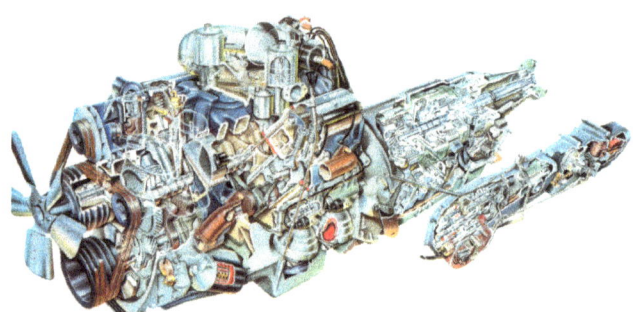

Engines are inherently reliable as long as they are well maintained. (Courtesy Rolls-Royce)

Examine the front floor of a car by lifting the carpet. If the underlay is wet, the moisture can rot the floorpan. (Courtesy SHRMF)

Advanced corrosion along the lower flanks of a car could be a reason to walk away from a deal!

Ideally, flexible hoses to the braking system should be renewed every 60,000 miles, along with disc brake caliper seals.

9 Serious evaluation

– 60 minutes for years of enjoyment

Circle the Excellent, Good, Average or Poor box of each section as you go along. The totting up procedure is detailed at the end of the chapter. **Be realistic in your markings!**

Exterior

Ex   Gd   Av   Po
4   3   2   1

Silver Shadows and Bentley Ts benefit from an excellent build quality, but vehicles which have not been maintained in accordance with the manufacturer's servicing schedules may display problems beneath a superficially grand exterior.

Bodywork and panels

Ex   Gd   Av   Po
4   3   2   1

Begin your tour of the car at the front of the vehicle, taking a look at the radiator shell, a magnificent item but expensive to repair. Silver Shadow and T bonnets (hoods) are not interchangeable.

A beautifully presented Series II Silver Shadow.

Owing to the upright contours of the frontal area, front panels are vulnerable to stones chipping the paintwork. Unless rectification work is immediately undertaken it is easy for rust to develop. A car showing signs of advanced decay in this respect will require extensive repairs, including a repaint. Look carefully at the condition of the paintwork around the air vents (according to model) beneath the headlights. Bubbling paint is a sign of rust beneath the skin, and it could well have broken through to the surface. Don't be fooled into thinking this will involve only minor rectification: once the paint has been removed, all sorts of problems can be exposed. Check the apron beneath the bumper for signs of corrosion. Series II vehicles have an air dam, so you'll need to check for any signs of rust or decay in this area. American specification vehicles were not fitted with air dams owing to the height of kerbs along sidewalks.

Bentley variants in good condition are particularly sought-after.

Now take a close look along the sides of the car, starting at the front and paying particular attention to the lower sections and wheelarches. Bodyshells were built to very high standards and it's unusual for them to rot throughout, the extent of serious decay being mainly confined to the lower area. At worst a car can display extensive rust around the wheelarches and along the sills to the extent that the metalwork has been completely eaten

Radiator shells are expensive to repair or replace, and front panels are vulnerable to stone chipping.

away. In such circumstances it's questionable whether an economical repair can be achieved, especially as the cost involved might be greater than the price of a car in relatively sound condition.

If evidence of repair work exists, it's essential to establish that the work was

Look for signs of bubbling paintwork around the front air vents.

On this Series II car, rot has extended from around the wheelarches to the sills, the metal having been eaten away.

This floorpan is sufficiently rotten for holes to appear.

In extreme cases the lower bodyshell aft of the rear wheelarches can become completely corroded.
(Courtesy Michael Hibberd)

undertaken by a specialist. Blistering of the paint around the wheelarches and along the sills could indicate that serious corrosion has taken a hold. The extent of any decay will dictate whether the entire wing has to be replaced or if it's possible to cut away the affected area and insert a repair section. New sills will have to replace those that are beyond repair.

Examine the chrome sections along the lower bodyshell. It's not uncommon to find signs of corrosion where the fastening clips go into the body. Finding evidence of rot at the bottom of the bodyshell, you should consider there also to be a problem with the floorpan. All Silver Shadows and Ts are vulnerable to windscreen leaks, the result being that moisture collects on the floorpan and is absorbed into the thick foam carpet underlay. At worst, the floorpan can completely rot away. The easiest way of checking the floorpan is to lift the carpeting in the front passenger compartment and examine the metal beneath. The extent of any corrosion to the lower section of the bodyshell will indicate whether an effective repair is possible.

Look for signs of corrosion along the lower edges of the bodywork aft of the rear wheelarches. Decay caught in its early stages can possibly be treated.

Soft-tops on convertible models should be examined carefully for wear or damage to the fabric and the efficient operation of the raising/lowering mechanism. Having checked the hood material, lower the top to the fully down position and check that the reservoir for the powered mechanism is full of fluid.

Paint

Ex 4 Gd 3 Av 2 Po 1

Damaged paintwork will not only be unsightly, it will be time consuming and expensive to rectify, especially if a bare metal repaint is necessary. Treat with caution a car that has recently been resprayed, by establishing why and when the work took place, and to whom entrusted. In the event of repairs following an accident, further investigation will be needed to establish the extent of damage and whether repairs were professionally undertaken.

Corrosion is evident where the moulding clips attach to the sill, and there is rot at the base of the wheelarch.

Shut lines

Ex 4 Gd 3 Av 2 Po 1

Examine the flanks of the vehicle to check whether the door shuts are even and flush with the bodywork. The distances between the shuts should be uniform, and doors that are proud, for example, along the bottom edges, should be checked for evidence of accident repair or deformation of the bodyshell. Look along the top edges to make sure they are level with the roofline.

The doors, bonnet and boot lid are formed from aluminium, but that doesn't mean they aren't prone to corrosion. Opening and closing the doors will reveal whether the rubbers are in good condition: the rubber seals along the back edge of the front doors are vulnerable to splitting, and evidence of this will require the rubbers to be replaced, at no small cost! The bonnet and boot shut lines should also be even, and do remember to check that the rubber seals around the boot are in place and in good condition.

Exterior trim

Ex 4 Gd 3 Av 2 Po 1

Replacement trim items are available but costly. Check the chrome fittings around the air vents below the headlights, and the high level mouldings along the doors, the latter not usually presenting a serious problem. Some cars were specified with 'Everflex' vinyl roof covering, and in this instance the material should be free from bulges or tears. Don't forget to check the condition of the chrome trim surrounding headlights, side and rear lamps, and external badging.

Doors should be easy to open and close, and shut lines even and flush.

Pitted chrome trimming can be expensive to replace.

Bumpers

Ex 4 Gd 3 Av 2 Po 1

Bumpers on Silver Shadows and Ts vary with model designation and market destination. Series I vehicles have chrome bumpers and overriders, while Series II cars, including the Corniche and Camargue, have a 'safety' design of bumper incorporating a polyurethane section. For the American market, USA safety legislation meant adoption, in 1973, of bumpers front and rear that were capable

... Likewise Series II type bumpers.

of absorbing minor impacts. This arrangement called for specially designed shock absorbers to be built behind the stainless steel frames to allow the bumpers to return to their original profile following an incident. UK and European market vehicles received a similar looking bumper on introduction of the Series II models, but were not energy absorbing in the American specification sense. All bumper components are expensive to repair or replace, the chrome quarter-sections on Series I models being vulnerable to rust as well as minor parking calamities.

The bumpers on this Series II car are damaged and ill-fitting.

Model designation

Ex	Gd	Av	Po
4	3	2	1

Model designation appears on the boot (trunk) lid. The R-R or winged B insignia is positioned directly above the combined boot lid catch and handle. Series I cars are designated Silver Shadow or T according to model. Corniche was applied to both Rolls-Royce and Bentley versions when introduced in 1971; the Camargue was only built as a Rolls-Royce, and was produced from 1975 until 1985. Second series cars were badged as Silver Shadow II and Bentley T2; the long wheelbase Silver Shadow became Silver Wraith II. The Corniche underwent several specification changes, thus the Corniche II was introduced in 1986 in America and in 1988 elsewhere; Corniche III arrived in 1990, Corniche IV in 1992, and Corniche S in 1995. The Bentley Corniche was renamed Continental in 1985.

The Corniche has the R-R or Bentley insignia on the bumper, and 'Corniche' on the boot lid.

Long wheelbase Rolls-Royce variants were badged Silver Wraith II.

Appropriate to variant, vehicles show the Rolls-Royce or Bentley insignia on the headlight assembly and instrumentation. Late Bentley Ts, of which few were built in comparison to the Silver Shadow, have instruments showing the R-R insignia.

The chassis serial number is stamped on the title plate on the left-hand side of the bulkhead, as well as being recorded at the front of the owner's handbook.

Windscreen wipers

These have two speeds and rarely give problems. Ensure that the blades are in good condition, and that the wash facility operates efficiently.

Lights

Ex	Gd	Av	Po
4	3	2	1

Camargue lighting.

All models have four-headlight systems, all lamps being of the sealed beam variety. The inner lamps provide long range illumination, the outer providing for dipped and wide-spread lighting. The inner lamps extinguish when dipped lighting is selected. Ensure that the headlights operate correctly, along with the foot-operated dipping mechanism. Check that side, tail and reversing

Rear lighting for Silver Shadow & T saloons – check that lenses are damage free, and that the surrounding trim is free from corrosion.

lights, along with direction indicators function correctly. Check that all lenses are secure and damage free. Camargues have elongated side lights and direction indicator units extending from beneath the headlights along the leading edges of the front wings. Headlight wash/wipe units when fitted are pivoted from the base in the case of Series II cars, and when fitted to the Camargue are top pivoted.

Wheels and tyres

Ex	Gd	Av	Po
4	3	2	1

When introduced the Silver Shadow was specified with cross-ply tyres, though most owners now fit radials. Radial tyres were officially specified from 1972, original tyre size was 8:15-15, pressures being 28psi front and rear, though when fully laden it was recommended pressures be 28psi front and 32psi rear. Avon tyres were usually specified, later cars having 235/70-15 radials with 24psi at the front and 28psi rear. As well as checking the depth of tread, look for splits or bulges in the sidewalls. Cars built before 1972 can show tyre wear on the inside edges, while later vehicles, those with compliant suspension, often have wear on the outer edges. Evidence

of feathering should be treated with caution as this could indicate problems associated with suspension or wheel balance. Don't expect to exceed much more than 15,000 miles from a set of tyres. Wheel trims have the R-R insignia and on T-series cars the Bentley name.

Hub bearings and steering joints

Ex [4] Gd [3] Av [2] Po [1]

To ensure longevity, it's recommended that front wheel bearings be repacked with grease every five years or 50,000 miles. Too much grease packed into a hub can result in brake disc contamination, thus causing obvious problems! Raise each wheel using the car's jack and investigate any rattling or looseness in the steering. This is a very specialised area and is best left to a marque specialist.

Check for looseness and wear or damage to the front hubs and steering joints. (Courtesy Michael Hibberd)

Look carefully for damage or tears to gaiters and seals.

Interior

Ex [4] Gd [3] Av [2] Po [1]

Apart from the style of facia, the interior of the standard steel saloons remained largely unchanged throughout the two series of cars. Even an early example of car that has been well maintained will retain its aura of luxury and continue to provide great satisfaction and pleasure. The coachbuilt variants, especially the Camargue, featured interiors crafted to even greater standards of luxury, often to customer specification. Stowage space within the cabin is adequate, there being shallow pockets in the front doors, a leather-trimmed glovebox in the facia, and deep pockets in the front seat backrests.

This early Silver Shadow has an interior with a nice patina.

An interior as nice as this has benefited from good maintenance.

Seats

Finished in Connolly hide, the seats should afford the greatest comfort and support. Caring owners will probably have kept the hide supple by use of 'hide feed', but don't be perturbed by seating which shows a distinctive patina. Seating with surface wear is arguably better than hides which have been subject to excessive 'Connollising'.

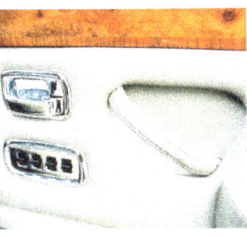

Trimming on a Silver Shadow or T is first class.

These seats require professional treatment, if they are to be saved!

Rear seats of the same car. The hide is stiff and needs careful restoration.

Seat operation switchgear is located on the central console of Series II cars. Note the worn condition of the hide.

Seat adjustment is electrically-operated for both forward and rearward movement; there is also independent height control to tilt either the front or rear of the seat base. On early cars the 8-position switchgear is located at the front edge of the centre armrest, on the central console on later models having the 'safety' facia, and on Series II vehicles the 'joystick' controls are positioned adjacent to the centre armrest ashtray. Rake adjustment is manually-operated via the lever situated on the outside edge of the seat base. Upholstery that is stained or damaged will need professional attention. The seat adjustment switchgear is very reliable, but it's essential to check that it operates correctly. Rear seat head restraints were fitted to Series II vehicles, but never to the front seats on UK and European market standard steel models. Front seat head restraints did feature on some American specification vehicles, as they did on later Corniche variants. According to model designation, some cars feature veneered picnic tables built into the front seat backrests. Ensure that the tables pull down freely and that all veneer surfaces are damage free. Rear compartment accessories include cigar lighters – check that these operate correctly.

Fuse board

This is the nerve centre of the car's electrical system; it's sensibly placed in a drop-down compartment located under the facia, above the brake pedal. It's clearly labelled, and there should be spare fuses along with a bobbin of fuse wire.

Fuse board is located beneath the facia and is complex in arrangement.

Carpeting

Ex 4   Gd 3   Av 2   Po 1

This is woven to the highest quality and has a thick underlay to afford a luxurious feel. The outer edges of the carpeting should not show signs of rot. Sheepskin carpet overlays were a popular accessory and, if fitted, should be clean and in good condition. Check, too, that the footrests for rear passengers are in place and free from damage and unsightly stains.

Floorpan

Ex 4   Gd 3   Av 2   Po 1

If the floor shows signs of corrosion it might be possible to plate it, but could mean fitting a whole new section, which is a major operation and could cast doubt on the viability of purchasing the vehicle.

A rotten front floorpan ...   ... and a rear floorpan that has rotted.

Headlining

Ex 4   Gd 3   Av 2   Po 1

Highest quality fabrics were used and should be in good condition.

Door locks and handles

Ex 4   Gd 3   Av 2   Po 1

These are of good quality and rarely give problems. The designs of door and boot handles vary according to whether the car is a standard steel vehicle or coachbuilt. Camargues have flush-fitting handles and locks.

Coachbuilt models have door handles to the coachbuilder's design, in this case Mulliner Park Ward.

Window winders

Ex 4   Gd 3   Av 2   Po 1

All vehicles are fitted with electrically-operated windows. Window lift motors, switchgear and mechanism are of good quality but can, on occasion, fail owing to the motors often having to operate in damp conditions.

Steering wheel

Ex 4   Gd 3   Av 2   Po 1

Series I cars were fitted with 16in steering wheels, Series II 15in. Two-spoke wheels were fitted to standard steel cars; some coachbuilt models have a three-spoke type.

Steering wheel design changed over the years; this is an early type. (Courtesy Rolls-Royce)

Facia and instrument board

On standard steel cars the facia design changed three times. The original style of facia was known within Rolls-Royce as the Chippendale owing to the extent of the woodwork. A new facia was introduced in 1969 to meet USA safety legislation and remained until introduction of the Series II vehicles in 1977. The 'safety' facia has thicker padding than the early type; there is also a centre console accommodating the air-conditioning outlet, radio, heating and ventilation controls, cigar lighter, and front seat adjustment switches. The third style of facia was introduced at the same time as the Series II vehicles and, with only minor alteration, was carried over to the Silver Spirit/Mulsanne family of cars when announced in 1980.

Facia as fitted to the earliest cars.

The post 1969 'safety' facia with its additional padding.

Series II facia, in this instance requiring restoration.

The facia and instrumentation adopted for the Camargue was different to that of the Silver Shadow/T.

The fine veneers are indicative of the craftsmanship that went into building the cars. Facias showing signs of damage will require specialist attention. As might be expected, these cars carry a comprehensive array of controls and instrumentation, all of which should be in good condition. Coachbuilt cars feature

This Bentley Convertible has the Mulliner Park Ward style of facia.

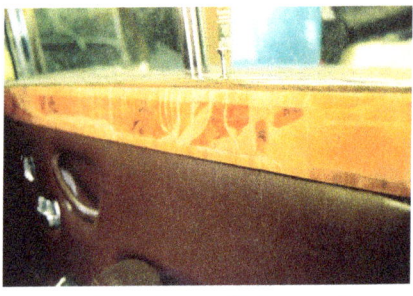

This is how a veneer should look ...

... but moisture has got in here and caused this opaque appearance.

styles of facia appropriate to the coachbuilder, and will, therefore, differ from the type fitted to standard steel models.

Facia and door capping veneers

Ex	Gd	Av	Po
4	3	2	1

These should be in good condition, but note evidence of lacquer having lifted or the ingress of moisture giving an opaque milky colour.

Rear companions

Ex	Gd	Av	Po
4	3	2	1

These are built into the rear quarters of the car and comprise a mirror and interior light to give an added touch of elegance.

Handbrake

Ex	Gd	Av	Po
4	3	2	1

This is mounted under the facia and is pulled towards the driver. When applied, the parking brake acts on the rear wheels, there being two pads on each

The handbrake lever can be obtrusive. Late models for the US market have a foot-controlled parking brake.

rear disc, which are self adjusting for wear. Turning the handle releases the brake.

Boot (trunk) interior

Ex	Gd	Av	Po
4	3	2	1

The luggage compartment is huge and well appointed. The battery compartment is located on the left-hand side of the boot, and should be concealed by removable trim. Check for any damage to the boot carpeting, especially around the battery, as acid fumes can rot the fabric. Pull away the battery cover and check the condition of the battery itself.

Spare wheel and tool kit

Ex	Gd	Av	Po
4	3	2	1

The spare wheel is mounted on a hinged platform beneath the boot floor. To lower the spare wheel from its location open the boot and undo the bolt found at the rear edge of the compartment, in the centre line of the vehicle, by using the box spanner tommy bar provided

The spare wheel is located beneath the boot floor. Look for corrosion on the rear apron when examining this area.

with the tool kit. Lifting the boot carpet will reveal a rubber cover which, when removed, allows the spare tyre to be inflated whilst in situ. The tool kit is located within the boot, the heavy items (jack, tommy bar and box spanner) being contained in a storage bag to the right-hand side of the compartment. The tommy bar also releases the wheel discs, and will operate the emergency gearbox selector fitted to early Series I vehicles. The box spanner fits the spare wheel platform, wheel nuts and sparking plugs. A small tool kit is located in the top of the battery box cover: remove the trim around the battery, place fingers in the grooves between the tool tray and slide out.

Mechanicals
Under the bonnet: general impressions

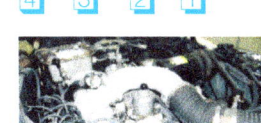

Ex   Gd   Av   Po
4   3   2   1

A neglected engine bay says a lot about a car.

The engine compartment is packed with pipework and trunking, not to mention the cooling system and the Rolls-Royce V8. Trunking should be in good condition (although it may look inexpensive, it's costly to replace). A well maintained car should show no evidence of water or anti-freeze leaks from the header tank or radiator. In the event of a header tank having to be replaced, this will prove to be very expensive. Look for general tidiness of the under-bonnet area, and note any signs of oil leakage. Check the oil, its condition and level (the dip-stick is on the left-hand side of the engine and is marked ENGINE): oil that is black and thick can suggest neglect. The oil filler is situated on the front face of the B cylinder head, i.e. right-hand side looking from the front of the car.

There is a myriad of pipes and wiring under the bonnet. Many owners entrust servicing to a specialist.

Engine

Ex   Gd   Av   Po
4   3   2   1

The Rolls-Royce V8 is beautifully engineered and, as long as it's used with respect and regularly maintained, will continue to give excellent service over many thousands of miles. The engine is common to all models, so expect to see Rolls-Royce stamped on the engine in the Bentley variants. An engine should not require major attention under 100,000 miles, but be warned that it might be difficult to diagnose any problems on high mileage cars from within the vehicle owing to the cars' smooth running and highly effective sound deadening. It is usual for the hydraulic tappets to be noisy when the engine is cold, but as soon as the

The V8 engine is beautifully-engineered and needs looking after. Tappets are noisy when the engine is cold. The diagram illustrates the lubrication system. (Courtesy Rolls-Royce)

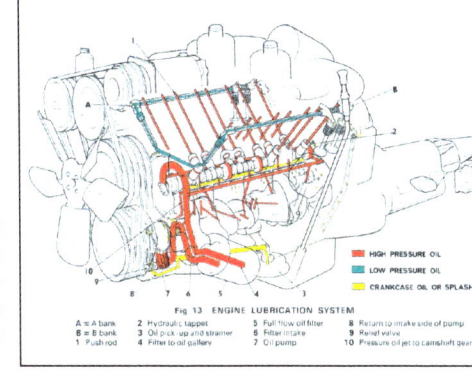

Fig 13 ENGINE LUBRICATION SYSTEM

unit warms the noise should disappear. Evidence of heavy knocking sounds when the engine is cold should be a cause for concern, especially as it's not unknown for pistons at the rear of the engine on Series II vehicles to seize. Should this happen, the cost of effecting repairs is enormous. Oil consumption should be minimal, so beware of an engine that requires constant topping up: check for evidence of leaks, and inspect the exhaust tailpipe for signs of burning oil.

Automatic transmission

Ex	Gd	Av	Po
4	3	2	1

Both the original four-speed and the later three-speed automatic gearboxes are reliable and, as long as a car has been treated with respect, will provide

Gearboxes are reliable, but check for leaks around the drain plug. (Courtesy Rolls-Royce)

excellent service. In order to check the gearbox fluid level, the engine must be running, the transmission set in 'P' (Park) mode, and the parking brake applied. The combined gearbox dip-stick and filler tube is located close to the bulkhead and is stamped 'GEARBOX'. Evidence of leakage or low gearbox fluid should be investigated.

The hydraulic system

Ex	Gd	Av	Po
4	3	2	1

This is a usually reliable but, nevertheless, highly complicated and important aspect of the car, and can be divided into three main sectors: the pressure generating circuit; the braking circuit; and self-levelling. The pressure generating circuit is comprised of three elements: fluid reservoir; hydraulic pump; and accumulator assembly. The fluid reservoir will need to be cleaned every two years, and provides fluid for the hydraulic system. The hydraulic pump forms the most important part of the system, while the accumulator regulates and restores pressure to the system as a whole.

Sight glasses in the hydraulic fluid reservoirs should be clean.

The self-levelling system is used by Rolls-Royce under licence from Citroën, but it is emphasised that the arrangement as fitted to the Silver Shadow and T is unlike that employed on Citroën's DS cars and their successors, inasmuch as it's employed for height control only and not the suspension system. Initially, the self-levelling was fitted to both the front and rear of the vehicle, but early on in production was removed from the front axle, leaving it to work solely at the rear.

Two types of fluid are employed for the hydraulic systems: from chassis 1001-49999 Castrol-Girling RR363 brake fluid was used; and from chassis 50000, Castrol-Girling mineral fluid. The fluids are not interchangeable and, should contamination occur in either system, rectification will be a specialist undertaking that is horribly expensive. With the bonnet open, check the hydraulic fluid levels through the sight glasses which, on a well maintained vehicle, will be clearly visible. If the level cannot be seen through the sight glasses this could indicate poor maintenance and that the fluid itself is old and dirty, thus in need of urgent replacement. Fluid is pumped around the hydraulic system at high pressure, is hygroscopic, and susceptible to dirt contamination. Levels of fluid can drop over time, but this should not happen as long as the system is regularly maintained and in good order. Evidence of low fluid level should be investigated, the initial course of action being to look for seepage around the sight glass seals, height control valves, or damaged brake pipes.

Brake pumps

Ex [4] Gd [3] Av [2] Po [1]

The brake pumps are an intrinsic part of the hydraulic system. To ensure they are operating correctly, the engine will need to have been running for several minutes. When the engine is warm depress the brake pedal about 15 times in quick succession to make the brake pumps work under load: there is every possibility they will emit a degree of noise, but only be concerned if the noise is inordinately loud. Switch off the engine and then turn on the ignition without restarting the engine: pump the brake pedal until the two low pressure brake warning lights illuminate on the instrument board. The system would appear to be in order if the lights illuminate after some twenty or more depressions; should they come on after only a few, say four or five, it is indicative of a problem with the brake accumulators, thus calling for specialist advice.

Engine and chassis numbers

Ex [4] Gd [3] Av [2] Po [1]

The engine serial number is stamped on the rear of the crankcase; chassis details can be found on the title plate on the left-hand side of the bulkhead.

Wiring

Ex [4] Gd [3] Av [2] Po [1]

Behind the instrument board the wiring assembly will appear almost too complex to comprehend! The switchgear is of high quality and should prove to be reliable, even on early vehicles.

This is the view behind the facia showing the wiring complexity!

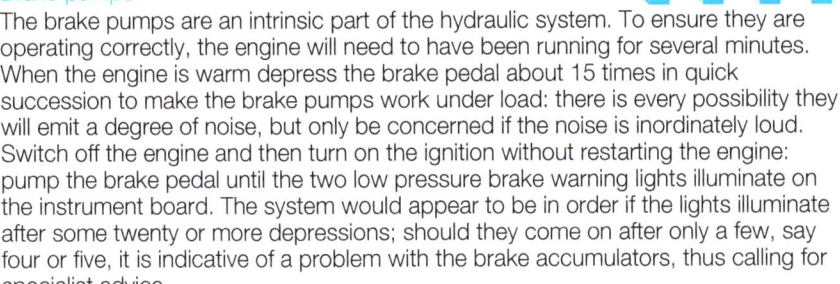

Hoses

Ex [4] Gd [3] Av [2] Po [1]

There is an abundance of hoses and pipework. All coolant hoses should be replaced every two years, an important practice as they deteriorate from the inside out. Any hoses that are limp or showing signs of deterioration should be replaced immediately.

Check hoses for damage; they are expensive to replace.

Cooling system

Ex [4] Gd [3] Av [2] Po [1]

It's good practice to drain and backflush the cooling system every two years or 25,000 miles. Unless a vehicle is to be used in very cold regions, the cooling system should comprise 50-50 water/anti-freeze. The thermostat should

Look for signs of leakage around the radiator.

also be replaced at the same time as the coolant. Take a look at the radiator filler cap: around the base there is a ridge which comes into contact with the seal, any damage, splitting or cracking will indicate that a new cap is required. The radiator itself should not show any signs of damage or leaks. The water pump should be checked for leaks, especially on high mileage cars. There is a hole beneath the water pump and ahead of the seal – any stains here would indicate the seal is leaking. Check the condition of the fanbelts, which should be changed every two years or 25,000 miles. Late models have as many as six belts.

Battery

Ex **4** Gd **3** Av **2** Po **1**

The battery has been dealt with in part elsewhere. The original specification was for a 64Ah unit; on introduction of the Series II vehicles, specification changed to 71Ah.

Carburettors and fuel injection

Ex **4** Gd **3** Av **2** Po **1**

Early cars were specified with twin SU HD8 carburettors, Series II vehicles with twin SU HIF7s. Fuel injection was specified on late Series II vehicles destined for the USA, though it was fitted to other market Corniche and Continental models from the mid-1980s.

Steering

Ex **4** Gd **3** Av **2** Po **1**

Nobody will argue that early models suffered from a vagueness of steering, something that was improved over the years, culminating in adoption of rack and pinion steering on Series II vehicles. Steering shafts and couplings on cars having a steering box (prior to Series II) should be checked closely. Look for the rubber coupling half way down the shaft which, if it's dry and cracked, will almost certainly cause some looseness and rattle in the steering system. Near to where the steering shaft attaches to the spool valve there is a Detroit trunnion joint and boot which, if torn, will allow dirt and moisture to contaminate the joint, thus causing its eventual failure. Steering boxes are very robust and rarely fail.

Check that steering joints are well lubricated.

Series II cars also have a rubber coupling on the steering shaft which can fail owing to becoming dry and cracked. The universal joints on Series II vehicles should also be checked for the same reason.

Check carefully the condition of the four bolts that attach the steering rack to the subframe. Should the bolts become loose, this can cause the legs of the steering rack to shear, with disastrous consequences. The convoluted boots on the steering rack could allow the ingress of dirt and moisture should they become damaged, thus calling for a major overhaul of the system.

Air-conditioning

Though air-conditioning was initially not a standard fitment, it was, in fact, a popular option. It was made standard in 1969, and in 1975 with the launch of the Camargue, an automatic split-level system was introduced and made available for the Corniche a year later and throughout the range of cars in 1977. On Series I cars, turn on the ignition and operate the heater switches so that, with every click of the switch, the electric motor can be heard running. If the system is working correctly, refrigerated air should be delivered from the bullseye vents on starting the engine.

The system is quite different on Series II cars, the controls comprising two wheels and a switch. With the engine running, the water temperature above 17 degrees centigrade, and the switch in the auto position – having chosen the desired temperature setting via the selector wheels – the servo will be heard operating until it has determined the required conditions. Should the system not be operational, suspect either a servo or sensor failure, both of which are likely to be expensive to correct.

Front and rear suspension

Inspection here is only really possble with the vehicle raised on a hoist or at the time of the road test. A car demonstrating all sorts of rattles, creaks and groans could well indicate that the suspension dampers are worn, and in this respect dampers can only be expected to last some 50,000 miles. If it's clear that the vehicle is overdue for damper replacement, the expense of undertaking this is likely to be high. In 1972, Rolls-Royce began to update the chassis, and introduced compliant suspension. The original 'Vibrashock' or 'pan-scrubber' subframe mountings were replaced with rubber mounts, and simultaneously the Panhard rod was discarded. The front track was also increased from 57.5in to 59.4in (1460/1511mm) and radial-ply and ventilated front discs were introduced, firstly on the Corniche but standardised in June 1973.

The general condition of the subframe should be checked for signs of damage, the Panhard rod on early cars should be secure, as should the nylon bushes at either end. The anti-roll bar bushes on the subframe should not appear worn,

Don't expect dampers to last more than 50,000 miles.

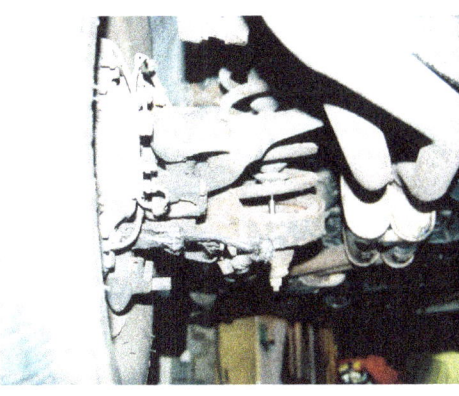

Coil spring replacement is a specialist operation.

the links (rubber ball joints) at the ends of the bar should not be lubricated or loose. Check the lower control levers, which are the point of greatest stress – wear here allows the bearing pin to rotate and thus the alignment to change. Check, too, the ball joints for splits which can allow the ingress of dirt and moisture.

When checking the rear suspension pay attention to the crossmember to which the trailing arms are connected. The compliance mounts can compress and so lose their ability to absorb any shocks. Look, too, at the tubular links that connect to the bottom of the crossmember, connecting to the body sill. If they are bent, they will require replacement. Any wear identified in the coil springs will need specialist attention as special tools are required for their removal and replacement.

Height control

Initially, vehicles were fitted with height control on both front and rear axles, but from August 1969 this was restricted to the rear axle. Few, if any, of the earliest cars remain in service with self-levelling to the front axle. Seven hydraulic units make up the self-levelling system of later cars: two height control valves, restrictors and rams, the latter being positioned in the front quarters of the boot (trunk) area and which maintain the ride height via the control valves. The restrictor valves control the manner in which the valves and rams operate, i.e. slowly or quickly according to variations in ride conditions. With the car in 'Park' or neutral, the system is on fast levelling; otherwise it's on slow. The height control system is usually reliable, but leaks can occur from the 'O' ring seal on the screwed section of the solenoid valve, which is an electrically-operated hydraulic valve which feeds fluid to the restrictor valve.

There is a test to ensure the system is operating correctly. With the engine running and transmission in neutral or Park, press down on the rear bumper; the hydraulics will react and raise the back of the car to its original height. Likewise, get someone to sit at the wheel and put the car into drive and press down on the rear of the car again – it should not return to the original position so quickly.

Brakes

Disc brakes are fitted all round, there being two twin-cylinder callipers fitted to each front wheel, and one four-cylinder calliper to each of the rear. The system comprises three separate and independent hydraulic circuits: two are power brake circuits; the third a master cylinder brake circuit. The master cylinder brake circuit comprises a master cylinder mounted at the rear of the foot pedal linkage and operates the lower pair of cylinders on each rear wheel calliper. The power brake circuit

Check the condition of the brake pads: if less than ¹⁄₁₆in of wear remains they must be changed. (Courtesy Rolls-Royce)

Fig 30   REAR DISC BRAKE

1 Power brake circuit bleed screw   4 Securing clip
2 Master cylinder circuit bleed screw   5 Locating pin
3 Disconnecting point   6 Hand brake pads
7 Adjusting ratchet seal

comprises two hydraulic pumps which are operated by the engine camshafts. When the brake pedal is applied, pressurised fluid is supplied to the front and rear wheel callipers, the pressure proportional to the load applied to the brake pedal.

The front and rear brakes are self-adjusting, but it's essential to check the condition of the brake pads every 6000 miles. Using the car's jack to raise the vehicle, and with a wheel removed, check the amount of wear left on the brake pad; it should not be less than $\frac{1}{16}$in. Check, too, that the friction material is uniform on all pads.

Inspect the brake discs for signs of corrosion or deformation, especially on a car that has been idle or laid-up for any length of time.

Test drive

Ex 4   Gd 3   Av 2   Po 1

See information given in Chapter 7 before embarking on a minimum 15 minute drive to evaluate the car's performance.

Ramp check

Ex 4   Gd 3   Av 2   Po 1

When taking a car for a test drive, listen for any undue noises coming from the engine or suspension. Don't let anyone deter you from investigating all potential problems.

Most exhaust/tyre centres will allow you to put a car on a ramp for a few minutes or so. You will need to look for accident damage to the underframes, deformation of the box sections, and for any serious oil leaks. Check the floorpan for signs of rust coming through from the interior. Any damage to the rear axle crossmember should be noted. Look at the condition of the outer universal joints of the drive shafts, in the event of damage replacement will be required. Check also the condition of brake lines, fuel pipes, the positive lead from the battery, exhaust system and petrol tank.

Evaluation procedure
Add up the total points score:
176 = excellent, possibly concours; 132 = good; 88 = average; 44 = poor.
Cars scoring over 123 will be completely useable and will require only maintenance and care to keep in condition. Cars scoring between 44 and 89 will require full restoration while cars scoring between 90 and 122 will require very careful assessment of necessary repair/restoration costs in order to reach a realistic value.

10 Auctions
– sold! Another way to buy your dream

Pros & cons
Pros: Prices will usually be lower than those of dealers or private sellers, and you might grab a real bargain. Auctioneers have usually established clear title with the seller. At the venue you can usually examine documentation relating to the vehicle.
Cons: You have to rely on a sketchy catalogue description of condition and history. The opportunity to inspect is limited, and you cannot drive the car. Auction cars are often a little below par and may require some work. It's easy to overbid. There will usually be a buyer's premium to pay in addition to the auction hammer price.

Which auction?
Auctions by established auctioneers are advertised in car magazines and on the auction houses' websites. A catalogue, or a simple printed list of the lots for auction might only be available a day or two ahead, though often lots are listed and pictured on auctioneers' websites much earlier. Contact the auction company to ask if previous auction selling prices are available, as this is useful information (details of past sales are often available on websites).

Catalogue, entry fee and payment details
When you purchase the auction catalogue, it often acts as a ticket allowing two people to attend the viewing days and the auction. Catalogue details tend to be comparatively brief, but will include such information as 'one owner from new, low mileage, full service history', etc. It will also usually show a guide price to give you some idea of what to expect to pay, and will tell you what is charged as a buyer's premium. The catalogue will also contain details of acceptable forms of payment.
    At the fall of the hammer an immediate deposit is usually required, the balance payable within 24 hours. If the plan is to pay by cash there may be a cash limit. Some auctions will accept payment by debit card. Sometimes credit or charge cards are acceptable, but will often incur an extra charge. A bank draft or bank transfer will have to be arranged in advance with your own bank as well as with the auction house. No car will be released before all payments are cleared. If delays occur in payment transfers then storage costs can accrue.

Buyer's premium
A buyer's premium will add to the hammer price – don't forget this in your calculations. It's not unusual for there to be a further state or local tax on top.

Viewing
In some instances it's possible to view on the day, or days before, as well as in the hours prior to, the auction. There are auction officials available who are willing to help out by opening engine and luggage compartments and to allow you to inspect the interior. While the officials may start the engine for you, a test drive is out of the question. Crawling under and around the car as much as you want is permitted, but you can't suggest that the car be jacked up, or attempt to do the job yourself. You can also ask to see any documentation available.

Bidding

Before you take part in the auction, decide your maximum bid – and stick to it!

It may take a while for the auctioneers to reach the lot you're interested in, so use that time to observe how other bidders behave. When it's the turn of your car, attract the auctioneer's attention and make an early bid. The auctioneer will then look to you for a reaction every time another bid is made, usually the bids will be in fixed increments until the bidding slows, when smaller increments will often be accepted before the hammer falls. If you want to withdraw from the bidding, make sure the auctioneer understands your intentions – a vigorous shake of the head when he or she looks to you for the next bid should do the trick! Assuming that you are the successful bidder, the auctioneer will note your paddle number, and from that moment on you will be responsible for the vehicle.

If the car is unsold, either because it failed to reach the reserve or because there was little interest, it may be possible to negotiate with the owner, via the auctioneers, after the sale is over.

Successful bid

There are two more items to think about: how to get the car home, and insurance. If you can't drive the car, your own or a hired trailer is one way, another is to have the vehicle shipped using the facilities of a local company. The auction house will also have details of companies specialising in the transfer of vehicles.

Insurance for immediate cover can usually be purchased on site, but it may be more cost-effective to make arrangements with your own insurance company in advance, and then call to confirm the full details.

eBay & other online auctions?

eBay & other online auctions could land you a car at a bargain price, though you'd be foolhardy to bid without examining it first, something most vendors encourage. A useful feature of eBay is that the geographical location of the car is shown, so you can narrow your choices to those within a realistic radius of home. Be prepared to be outbid in the last few moments of the auction. Remember, your bid is binding, and it will be very, very difficult to get restitution in the case of a crooked vendor fleecing you – caveat emptor!

Be aware that some cars offered for sale in online auctions are 'ghost' cars. Don't part with any cash without being sure that the vehicle does actually exist and is as described (usually pre-bidding inspection is possible).

Auctioneers

Barrett-Jackson	www.barrett-jackson.com
Bonhams	www.bonhams.com/cars
British Car Auctions (BCA)	www.bca-europe.com or www.british-car-auctions.co.uk
Cheffins	www.cheffins.co.uk
Christies	www.christies.com
Coys	www.coys.co.uk
eBay	www.ebay.com
H&H	www.handh.co.uk
RM	www.rmauctions.com
Shannons	www.shannons.com.au
Silver	www.silverauctions.com

11 Paperwork
– correct documentation is essential!

The paper trail

Rolls-Royces and Bentleys are usually accompanied by a large portfolio of paperwork, accumulated and passed on by a succession of proud owners. This documentation, which might include copies of the original factory records, represents the real history of the car, and from it can be deduced the level of care the car has received, how much it's been used, which specialists have worked on it, and the dates of major repairs and restorations. All this information is priceless to you as the new owner, so be very wary of cars with little or no paperwork to support their claimed history.

Registration documents

All countries/states have some form of registration for private vehicles, whether it's like the American 'pink slip' system or the British 'log book' arrangement. It's essential to check that the registration document is genuine, that it relates to the car in question, and that all the vehicle's details are correctly recorded, including chassis/VIN and engine numbers (if these are shown). If you're buying from the previous owner, his or her name and address will be recorded in the document – this will not be the case if you're buying from a dealer.

In the UK, the current (Euro-aligned) registration document is named 'V5C', and is printed in coloured sections of blue, green and pink. The blue section relates to the car's specification, the green section has details of the new owner, and the pink section is sent to the DVLA in the UK when the car is sold. A small section in yellow deals with selling the car within the motor trade.

In the UK, the DVLA will provide details of former keepers of the vehicle upon payment of a small fee, and much can be learned in this way.

If the car has a foreign registration there may be expensive and time-consuming formalities to complete. Do you really want the hassle? Silver Shadows and Bentley Ts sometimes wear personalised plates which the owner wants to transfer to another vehicle, so the car will require a new, age-related, registration. It's possible that you already have a personalised plate that you want to transfer to your acquisition; in any event you'll have to negotiate with your licensing authority.

Roadworthiness certificate

Most country/state administrations require that vehicles are regularly tested to prove that they are safe to use on the public highway, and do not produce excessive emissions. In the UK that test (the MoT) is carried out at approved testing stations, for a fee. In the USA, the requirement varies, but most states insist on an emissions test every two years as a minimum, while the police are charged with pulling over unsafe-looking vehicles.

In the UK, the test is required on an annual basis once a vehicle becomes three years old. Of particular relevance for older cars is that the certificate issued includes the mileage reading recorded at the test date, and this, therefore, becomes an independent record of that car's history. Ask the seller if previous certificates are available. Without an MoT the vehicle should be trailored to its new home, unless you insist that a valid MoT is part of the deal (not such a bad idea this, as at least you'll know the car was roadworthy on the day it was tested and you don't need to wait for the old certificate to expire before having the test done.)

Road licence

The administration of every country/state charges some kind of tax for the use of its road system, the actual form of the 'road licence' and how it is displayed, varying enormously country-to-country and state-to-state.

Whatever the form of the 'road licence', it must relate to the vehicle carrying it, and must be present and valid if the car is to be driven legally on the public highway. The value of the licence will depend on the length of time it will continue to be valid. In the UK, if a car is untaxed because it has not been used for a period of time, the owner has to inform the licensing authorities, otherwise the vehicle's date-related registration number will be lost and there will be a painful amount of paperwork to get it re-registered. Also in the UK, vehicles built before the end of 1972 are provided with 'tax discs' free of charge, but they must still display a valid disc. Car clubs can often provide formal proof that a particular car qualifies for this valuable concession.

Certificates of authenticity

The Rolls-Royce Enthusiasts' Club can provide copies of factory records for all Silver Shadows and Bentley Ts for a fee, so a particular vehicle's age and authenticity can be proved (e.g. engine and chassis numbers, paint colour, upholstery and veneer details), which is a definite bonus. If you want to obtain these details, the R-REC is the best starting point.

If the car has been used in European classic car rallies it may have a FIVA (Federation Internationale des Vehicules Anciens) certificate. The so-called 'FIVA Passport', or 'FIVA Vehicle Identity Card', enables organisers and participants to recognise whether or not a particular vehicle is suitable for individual events. If you want to obtain such a certificate go to www.fbhvc.co.uk or www.fiva.org; there will be similar organisations in other countries, too.

Valuation certificate

Hopefully, the vendor will have a recent valuation certificate, or letter signed by a recognised expert stating how much he, or she, believes the particular car to be worth (such documents, together with photos, are usually needed to get 'agreed value' insurance). Generally speaking, such documents should act only as confirmation of your own assessment of the car rather than a guarantee of value, as the expert has probably not seen the car in the flesh. The easiest way to find out how to obtain a formal valuation is to contact the R-REC.

Service history

Often these cars will have been serviced by specialist firms or marque dealers over a good number of years. Nevertheless, try to obtain as much service history and other paperwork pertaining to the car as you can. Naturally, dealer stamps, or specialist garage receipts score most points in the value stakes. However, anything helps in the great authenticity game – items like the original bill of sale, handbook, parts invoices and repair bills, adding to the story and the character of the car. Even a brochure correct to the year of manufacture is a useful document, and is something that you could well have to search hard to locate in future years. If the seller claims that the car has been restored, then expect receipts and other evidence from a specialist restorer.

If the seller claims to have carried out regular servicing, ask what was completed, when, and seek some evidence of it being carried out. Your assessment of the car's overall condition should tell you whether the seller's claims are genuine.

Restoration photographs

If the seller tells you that the car has been restored, then expect to be shown a series of photographs taken while the restoration was underway. Pictures taken at various stages, and from various angles, should help you gauge the thoroughness of the work. If you buy a car, ask if you can have all the photographs as they form an important part of the vehicle's history. It's surprising how many sellers are happy to part with their car and accept your cash, but want to hang on to their photographs! In the latter event, you may be able to persuade the vendor to get a set of copies made.

This publicity photograph of the Corniche was aimed at the American market. (Courtesy Rolls-Royce)

12 What's it worth to you?

– let your head rule your heart!

Condition

By using this book you should know whether the car is in Excellent (maybe concours), Good, Average or Poor condition.

Many classic/collector car magazines run a regular price guide. If you haven't bought the latest editions, do so now, and compare their suggested values for the model you're thinking of buying – also look at the auction prices they're reporting. Values have been fairly stable for some time, but some models will always be more sought-after than others. Trends can change too. The values published in the magazines tend to vary from magazine to magazine, as do their scales of condition, so carefully read the guidance notes they provide. Bear in mind that a car that is truly a recent show winner could be worth more than the highest scale published. Assuming that the car you have in mind is not in show/concours condition, then relate the level of condition that you judge the car to be in with the appropriate guide price. How does the figure compare with the asking price? Before you start to haggle with the seller, consider what effect any variation from standard specification might have on the car's value.

If you're buying from a dealer, remember there will be a premium on the price.

Desirable options/extras

Being of such prestigious nature, the Silver Shadow and T-series cars were specified with every conceivable luxury and, therefore, there was a limit to the number of optional extras. Owing to criticism regarding the early cars' handling, two handling kits intended to improve matters were offered: one factory-approved; the other by Harvey-Bailey Engineering. Both kits successfully improve handling characteristics and can be fitted retrospectively.

Owing to the number of modifications made to these cars during their production, many potential buyers opt for the second series cars. Compared to the standard saloons, the coachbuilt models display an even higher level of luxury. It was possible to specify rear-compartment foot rests and sheepskin or deep pile lambswool overrugs, all of which add a touch of sophistication and even greater luxury. Everflex roofs were a popular option, as was two-tone paintwork.

Undesirable features

Retrospectively-fitted driving lamps, customisation, and items that are non-standard will not look right. Upholstery that has been allowed to fall into neglect will present a poor image, and vehicles with instruments missing, damaged or faulty should be regarded with suspicion.

Striking a deal

Negotiate on the basis of your condition assessment, mileage, and fault rectification cost. Also take into account the car's specification. Be realistic about the value, but don't be completely intractable: a small compromise on the part of the vendor or buyer will often facilitate a deal at little real cost.

13 Do you really want to restore?
– it'll take longer and cost more than you think

Ask anyone with experience of restoring a Silver Shadow or T-series and you'll get a quick response – don't attempt it! That said, a number of marque enthusiasts have carried out a full restoration of their cars, and can proudly demonstrate the result of their efforts.

Restoring one of these cars is a mammoth operation, calling for great expense and time. The prospect of undertaking such a task has to be very carefully considered in respect of resources. You'll need space to move around the vehicle, strip it down, and reach some of the more inaccessible components. Then

Silver Shadows & Ts are complex cars – get to know where everything is! (Courtesy Michael Hibberd)

there's having somewhere to store the parts, and a workbench on which to clean and renovate those items that can be salvaged.

Before embarking upon a restoration project you would be wise to familiarise yourself with the car's complex engineering and construction. Acquisition of an official Rolls-Royce workshop manual is essential, and you'll find that some of the jobs involved in the rebuilding process require costly special tools.

Whilst there is a specialist industry devoted to preserving these cars, you have to ask yourself what degree of restoration you'd be happy with. Can you live with fitting used and recycled components? Will you be satisfied with anything less than sheer perfection? If items such as wings, doors, bonnet, boot lid, and radiator grille, etc, are beyond repair, it will be necessary to obtain new components, or at least those that are second-hand but in such good condition that they can be utilised with the minimum of renovation.

Consider, too, that the bodywork will need careful and expert preparation before repainting. Certain other aspects of restoration will have to be entrusted to specialist craftsmen, e.g. woodwork and upholstery, and then there's the vehicle's hydraulics, including the self-levelling system. Don't forget the electrics and air-conditioning; these are intricate parts of the car.

Undertaking a restoration project is likely to be more costly than even the most careful budgeting predicted. Delays will be inevitable, and there's the possibility of

Restoring a car to pristine condition can often cost more than buying a vehicle that is in a reasonable state of repair. (Courtesy Michael Hibberd)

the whole affair becoming such a burden that you'll lose interest in the venture: it happens. On the other hand, acquiring a particular coachbuilt example, or a car that has historical interest, might have appeal. If, however, it's your intention to have a car professionally restored, this might be the most acceptable approach, as long as the astronomical cost is acceptable.

In summary, restoring a Silver Shadow or Bentley T is not for those with limited skills when it comes to automotive know-how. Spending more money in the first instance to buy a first class example of car that is useable, even award-winningly pristine, could be more satisfying in the long run. What's more, you'll have a car to enjoy to its full potential!

Items like window lift motors can be expensive; second-hand equipment might require renovation before use.

Restoring a car's interior requires specialist attention, and achieving Rolls-Royce quality is pricey.

14 Paint problems

The paintwork on a Silver Shadow and Bentley T is probably the best you'll find on any car, and its quality is due to a painstaking preparation process that ensured a legendary finish. Paint faults generally occur due to lack of protection/maintenance, or to poor preparation prior to a respray or touch-up. Some of the following conditions may be present in the car you're looking at:

Orange peel
This appears as an uneven paint surface, similar to the appearance of the skin of an orange. The fault is caused by the failure of atomized paint droplets to flow into each other when they hit the surface. It's sometimes possible to rub out the effect with proprietary paint cutting/rubbing compound or

A fault such as this suggests evidence of an economy repair, and something sinister beneath the paint.

very fine grades of abrasive paper. However, a respray may be necessary in severe cases. Consult a bodywork repairer/paint shop for advice on the particular car.

Cracking
Severe cases are likely to have been caused by too heavy an application of paint (or filler beneath the paint). Also, insufficient stirring of the paint before application can lead to the components being improperly mixed, and cracking can result. Incompatibility with the paint already on the panel can have a similar effect. To rectify the problem it will be necessary to rub down to a smooth, sound finish before respraying the problem area.

Crazing
Sometimes the paint takes on a crazed rather than a cracked appearance when the problems mentioned under 'cracking' are present. This problem can also be caused by a reaction between the underlying surface and the paint. Paint removal and respraying the area is usually the only solution.

Paint cracking has appeared on this front wheelarch.

Blistering
Almost always caused by corrosion of the metal beneath the paint. Usually perforation will be found in

Stone chips have caused the paint to blister here.

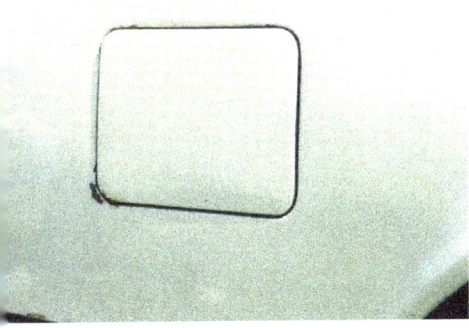

Blistering paintwork left unchecked has already allowed the metal beneath to corrode further.

the metal, and the damage will usually be worse than that suggested by the area of blistering. The metal will have to be repaired before repainting.

Micro blistering

Usually the result of an economy respray where inadequate heating has allowed moisture to settle on the car before spraying. Consult a paint specialist, but usually damaged paint will have to be removed before partial or full respraying. Can also be caused by car covers that don't 'breathe'.

Fading

Some colours, especially reds, are prone to fading if subject to strong sunlight for long periods without the benefit of polish protection. Sometimes proprietary paint restorers and/or paint cutting/rubbing compounds will retrieve the situation. Often a respray is the only real solution.

Peeling

Often a problem with metallic paintwork when the sealing lacquer becomes damaged and begins to peel off. Poorly applied paint may also peel. The remedy is to strip and start again!

Dimples

Dimples in the paintwork are caused by the residue of polish (particularly silicone types) not being removed properly before respraying. Paint removal and repainting is the only solution.

Dents

Small dents are usually easily cured by the 'Dentmaster', or equivalent process, that sucks or pushes out the dent (as long as the paint surface is still intact). Companies offering dent removal services usually come to your home – consult your telephone directory or the internet.

Minor dents in this Camargue could prove difficult to rectify.

15 Problems due to lack of use

– just like their owners, Silver Shadows/Ts need exercise!

Cars, like humans, need regular exercise, and a run of at least ten miles once a week is recommended for classics.

Seized components

Pistons in brake calipers, slave and master cylinders can seize. Handbrakes (parking brakes) can seize if the cables and linkages rust. Pistons can seize in the engine's bores due to corrosion.

Fluids

Old, acidic oil can corrode bearings. Uninhibited coolant can corrode internal waterways, and lack of anti-freeze can have the effect of pushing out core plugs or causing damage to the cylinder block and heads. If silt has settled or solidified the result will be overheating.

Brake fluid absorbs water from the atmosphere and should be renewed every two years. Old fluid with a high water content can cause corrosion and pistons/callipers to seize (freeze) and can cause brake failure when the water turns to vapour near hot braking components.

Fluids, especially in respect of a Rolls-Royce's hydraulic system, require careful attention. The state of this reservoir indicates the entire system will need overhauling before use.

Tyres

Tyres that have the weight of a car on them in a single position for some time will develop flat spots, resulting in some (usually temporary) vibration. The tyre walls may have cracks or (blister-type) bulges, meaning new tyres are needed.

Shock absorbers (dampers)

As well as a conventional suspension, the Silver Shadow/T has hydraulic self-levelling. With lack of use the dampers will lose their elasticity or may seize, while the self-levelling system may become inoperative due to leakage of fluid or component seizure.

Tyres on a car not used in a long time could lead to an MoT failure. Hoses might have perished and brake calipers seized.

Rubber and plastic
Radiator hoses may have perished and split, possibly resulting in loss of coolant. Check the condition of door and boot rubbers, which might be hardened and split, windscreen wiper blades will have hardened with age.

Electrics
The battery will be of little use if not charged for many months and may well be damaged. Earthing/grounding problems are common when the connections have corroded. Old bullet or spade type electrical connectors commonly rust/corrode and will need disconnecting, cleaning and protection (e.g. Vaseline). Sparkplug electrodes will often have corroded in an unused engine. Wiring insulation can harden and fail. The battery is situated in the boot, check its condition and check also that the acid fumes have not rotted the carpet.

Exhaust systems
Exhaust gas contains a high water content so exhaust systems corrode very quickly from inside when the car is not used.

Interior
A vehicle left standing for a long period in a poorly ventilated area may develop a musty smelling interior: upholstery might become damp, veneers can deteriorate and carpets rot.

A car's interior will suffer if neglected during long-term storage; wiring and switches may deteriorate.

16 The Community
– key people, organisations and companies in the Silver Shadow/T world

The Rolls-Royce and Bentley community is worldwide. Bentley Motors has responsibility for the supply of parts, through its dealerships, of all genuine 'Crewe' spares, but there are numerous independent specialists (including those who are members of the Rolls-Royce & Bentley Specialists Association) which supply parts, new, used or recycled, and which are involved in the maintenance and restoration of vehicles.

The clubs

Rolls-Royce and Bentley enthusiasts are supported internationally by a number of organisations. In the United Kingdom, these are the Rolls-Royce Enthusiasts' Club (R-REC) and the Bentley Drivers Club (BDC). The R-REC has localised sections within the United Kingdom, throughout Western Europe, and in Hong Kong, Japan, South Africa and Canada. An intrinsic aspect of the R-REC is its technical support, which includes practical help seminars.

The Rolls-Royce Enthusiasts' Club caters for all Rolls-Royce cars and those Bentleys built after 1931. Headquarters of the R-REC is located at The Hunt House, High Street, Paulerspury, near Towcester in Northamptonshire, and in addition to providing the organisation's administrative affairs, houses a huge collection of archives and build histories of all Rolls-Royces and post-1931 Bentleys. R-REC members receive the excellent bi-monthly Bulletin. The monthly Advertiser carries classified advertisements on behalf of marque specialists, as well as vehicles offered for sale by individual members. Contact: telephone 01327 811788; fax 01327 811797; shop 01327 811489. Email:admin@rrec.org.uk; web site http//www.rrec.co.uk

Rolls-Royce and Bentley communities are alive and well. (Courtesy SHRMF)

The BDC, too, is international, linking UK members with enthusiasts in Europe, America, Australia, Japan and South Africa. Autonomous clubs are to be found throughout America, Australia and New Zealand. The BDC's headquarters at the WO Bentley Memorial Building, Ironstone Lane, Wroxton, Banbury, Oxfordshire maintains an extensive collection of archives, though members may have to apply to view them. All Bentley enthusiasts are welcomed and there is technical help available. Members receive the excellent bi-monthly *Review* along with the monthly *Preview and Advertiser*. Contact: BDC Club Office, telephone 01622 858361; fax 01295 738887 (www.bdcl.org; email, info@bdcl.org).

Clubs outside the UK
America
The Rolls-Royce Owners Club (R-ROC). Tel 717 6974671; fax 717 6977820; email rrochq@rroc.org

Australia
Rolls-Royce Owners' Club of Australia (RROCA). Contact via website, http://rroc.org.au

New Zealand
New Zealand Rolls-Royce & Bentley Club Inc. Tel (09) 238 4487; email Ralph.Atkinson@blennz.school.nz

Books and workshop manuals
Rolls-Royce Silver Shadow/Bentley T-Series, Camargue & Corniche (ISBN 978-1-904788-25-4), written by the author of this guide and available from Veloce Publishing (as well as the R-REC and BDC shops), traces the origins of the cars, their development and production history. A companion volume, *Rolls-Royce Silver Spirit & Silver Spur, Bentley Mulsanne, Eight, Continental, Brooklands & Azure – Updated & enlarged Second Edition* (ISBN 978-1-904788-75-1), again by the same author is also available. *Rolls-Royce Silver Wraith, Silver Dawn & Silver CloudBentley MkVI, R-Series & S-Series* (ISBN 978-1-874105-87-9) by Martyn Nutland, is also available from Veloce.

Both the R-REC and BDC through their respective club shops sell a wide selection of Rolls-Royce and Bentley literature. Workshop manuals for the Silver Shadow and T-series are also available from the R-REC.

For an up-to-date list of marque specialists contact the relevant enthusiast club or consult the internet.

17 Vital statistics
– essential data at your fingertips

Production figures

Silver Shadow cars	37,971
Bentley T cars	2585
Total	**40,556**

Performance (all Series I models): Maximum speed 115mph (185kph)
Fuel consumption: 11-15mpg (25.7lt/100km-18.8lt/100km, average 12.2mpg (23.2lt/100km)
Silver Shadow II/ T2/SWII and T2 LWB: 119mph (190.4kph); 13.6mpg (20lt/100km)
Corniche/Camargue: 120mph (192kph); 11.9mpg (24lt/100km)

Engine
6230cc: ohv V8 with hydraulic tappets. Bore 4.1in (104.14mm), stroke 3.6in (91.44mm). Compression ratio 9.0:1.
6750cc: Bore 4.1in (104.14mm), stroke 3.9in (99.1mm). Compression ratio 9:1; from 1975 compression ratio changed to 8:1, and 7.3:1 for American, Australian and Japanese markets.

Transmission
Home market cars fitted with 4-speed automatic transmission, left-hand export models had GM400 3-speed gearbox. The GM400 gearbox became standard on all models after 1968.

Brakes
Disc brakes fitted all round. The parking brake is manually-operated.

Electrics
12-volt negative earth, 64Ah battery (71Ah Series II).

Dimensions
Silver Shadow T

Wheelbase	9ft 11.75in (3035mm)
Track, front and rear	4ft.9in (1460mm)
Ground clearance	6.5in (1650mm)
Turning circle	38ft (11,580mm)
Overall length	16ft 11.5in (5170mm)
Overall width	5ft 11in (1800mm)
Overall height	4ft 11.75in (1520mm)
Variations	Long wheelbase Series I models
Wheelbase	10ft 3.5in (3035mm)
Overall length	17ft 3.5in (5270mm)

Silver Shadow II and T2

Track, front	5ft (1524mm), rear 4ft 11.5in (1514mm)

56

Overall length	17ft 0.5in (5194mm)
Overall width	5ft 11.75in (1820mm)
Turning circle	39ft 2in (11,938mm)

Silver Wraith II/T2LWB

Wheelbase	10ft 3.5in (3035mm)
Track, rear	4ft 11.5in (1514mm)
Overall length	17ft 4.5in (5296mm)
Turning circle	39ft 2in (11,938mm)

Corniche

Wheelbase	as for saloon
Track, front and rear	4ft 9.5in (1460mm)
Overall length	17ft 3.5in (5270mm)
Overall width	6ft (1830mm)
Turning circle	38ft 9in (11,811mm)

Camargue

Wheelbase	9ft 11.75in (3035mm)
Track	front and rear 4ft 9.5in (1460mm)
Overall length	16ft 11.5in (5169mm)
Overall width	6ft 3.5in (1918mm)
Turning circle	38ft 6in (11,735mm)

Other models

Overall length	North American Silver Shadow II, 17ft 3.5in (5270mm); North American Silver Wraith II, 17ft 8.5in (5397.5mm)

Weights

Silver Shadow and T full tank of fuel LWB models	unladen, complete with oil, coolant, and
Silver Shadow and T	4760lb (2159kg)
LWB models	5010lb (2275kg)
Silver Shadow II and T2	4930lb (2237kg)
Silver Wraith II andT2 LWB	5020lb (2277kg)
Silver Wraith II with division	5260lb (2358kg)
Two-door saloon	4978lb (2258kg)
Two-door convertible	5124lb (2322kg)
Corniche saloon	5045lb (2288kg)
Corniche convertible	5200lb (2358kg)
Camargue	5175lb (2347kg)

Capacities

Fuel tank	23.5 imp galls, 28.8 US galls, 109 litres. Fuel tank later increased to 24imp galls
Engine oil	14 imp pints, 16.8 US pints, 8.0 litres
Gearbox oil	24 imp pints, 28.8US pints, 13.6 litres
Coolant	28 imp pints, 33.6US pints, 16 litres

Wheels and tyres
15in, 5-stud steel wheels, 8.45x15 low profile tyres

Major specification changes
1966: James Young introduced a two-door saloon; Mulliner Park Ward (MPW) introduced 'official' 2-door model the same year
1968: GM400 gearbox became standard on all cars (chassis 4483)
1969: LWB saloon introduced
1970: Engine size increased from 6.25 to 6.75 litres. Central locking standardised
1971: Corniche introduced
1972: Suspension modified – now 'compliant'. Radial tyres specified
1973: North American cars have energy absorbing bumpers and pedal-operated parking brake. Ventilated front disc brakes
1974: Wheelbase extended, wider section tyres fitted, wheelarches flared
1975: Electronic ignition specified. Camargue introduced featuring automatic split level air-conditioning
1976: Corniche receives automatic split level air-conditioning
1977: Silver Shadow II and T2 introduced; rack and pinion steering specified
1979: Suspension revised on Corniche and Camargue
1980: Bosch fuel injection introduced on Camargue and Corniche. Silver Shadow II and T2 discontinued
1985: Bentley Corniche renamed Continental
1986: Corniche II introduced for North America
1990: Corniche III introduced
1992: Corniche IV introduced
1995: Corniche S and Bentley Continental Turbo available. Last Corniche models built

Key model changes by chassis number
3000	Saginaw power steering pump introduced
4469	Revised handbrake
6429	Higher steering ratio
6771	New road wheels
8222	Smaller diameter steering wheel
4483	GM400 gearbox fitted
7404	Forward height control deleted
7500	Alternator replaces dynamo; air-conditioning standard
7620	Stainless steel exhaust standard
8742	6.75 litre engine introduced
9658	Central locking
11130	Synthetic hydraulic fluid specified
11466	Long stroke front dampers
13485	Compliant suspension introduced
15950	Front disc brakes now ventilated
18269	Flared wheel arches on saloon, 18563 on Corniche
22118	Brake master cylinder discontinued; electronic ignition introduced
30001	Series II models introduced

The Silver Shadow and T were unveiled to Rolls-Royce and Bentley dealers on 30th September and 1st November 1965, respectively, at the Crewe factory. Development of the cars was conducted over a period of ten years, the Bentley originally planned as a smaller car to the Silver Shadow. Ultimately, the Bentley design was adopted for both marques. (Courtesy Rolls-Royce)

On 13th May 1996, some thirty years after the Silver Shadow's and T's introduction, John Blatchley (right) is reunited with the car he designed. Rolls-Royce's former Chief Stylist is accompanied by his senior stylists, Bill Allen (left) and Martin Bourne, the location being The Hunt House, the Paulerspury (Northamptonshire) HQ of the Rolls-Royce Enthusiasts' Club.

The Essential Buyer's Guide™ series ...

... don't buy a vehicle until you've read one of these!

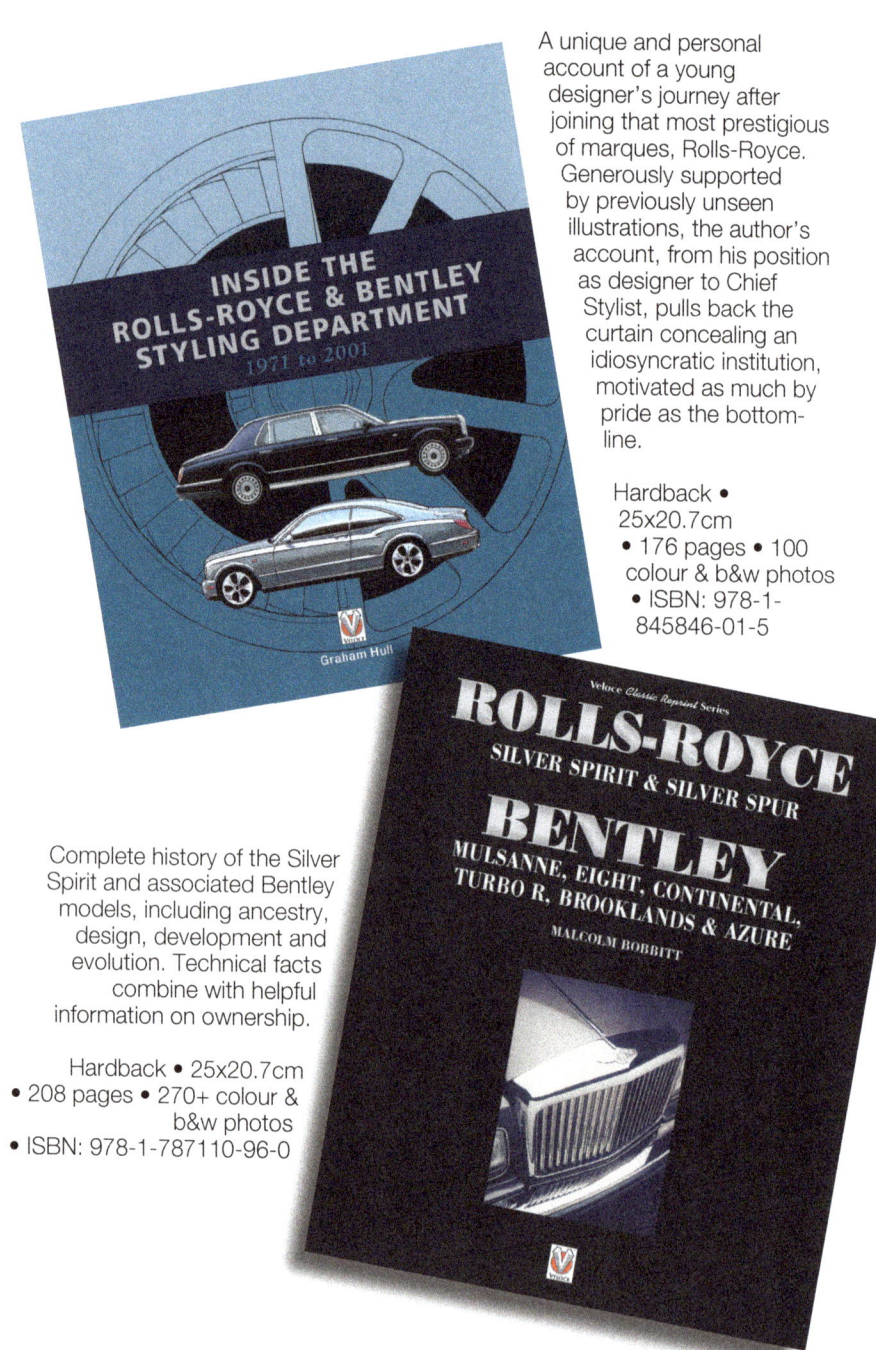

A unique and personal account of a young designer's journey after joining that most prestigious of marques, Rolls-Royce. Generously supported by previously unseen illustrations, the author's account, from his position as designer to Chief Stylist, pulls back the curtain concealing an idiosyncratic institution, motivated as much by pride as the bottom-line.

Hardback •
25x20.7cm
• 176 pages • 100
colour & b&w photos
• ISBN: 978-1-
845846-01-5

Complete history of the Silver Spirit and associated Bentley models, including ancestry, design, development and evolution. Technical facts combine with helpful information on ownership.

Hardback • 25x20.7cm
• 208 pages • 270+ colour &
b&w photos
• ISBN: 978-1-787110-96-0

The development and production history of the elegant and luxurious mainstream Rolls-Royce and Bentley models built between 1947 and 1965.

Hardback • 25x20.7cm • • 176 pages • Over 160 colour & b&w photos • ISBN: 978-1-84584-068-6

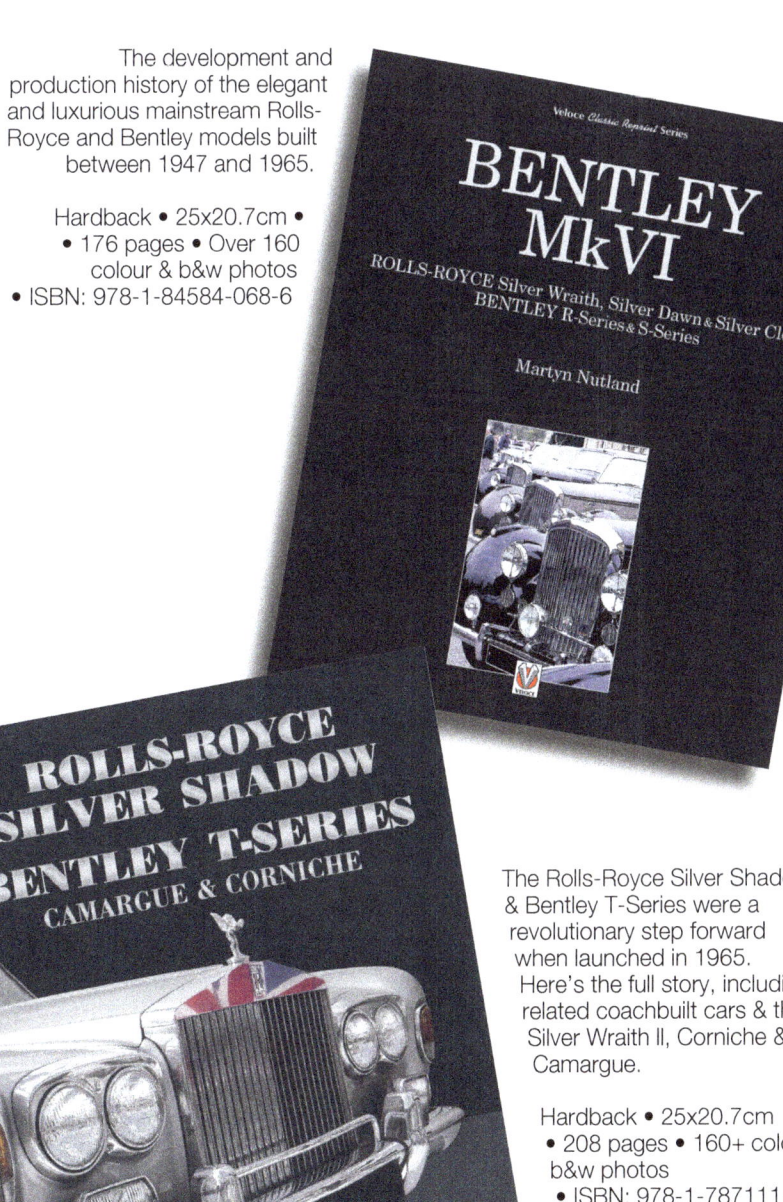

Veloce *Classic Reprint* Series

BENTLEY MkVI

ROLLS-ROYCE Silver Wraith, Silver Dawn & Silver Cloud BENTLEY R-Series & S-Series

Martyn Nutland

ROLLS-ROYCE SILVER SHADOW BENTLEY T-SERIES CAMARGUE & CORNICHE

UPDATED FOURTH EDITION

The Rolls-Royce Silver Shadow & Bentley T-Series were a revolutionary step forward when launched in 1965. Here's the full story, including related coachbuilt cars & the Silver Wraith II, Corniche & Camargue.

Hardback • 25x20.7cm • 208 pages • 160+ colour & b&w photos • ISBN: 978-1-787111-37-0

Index